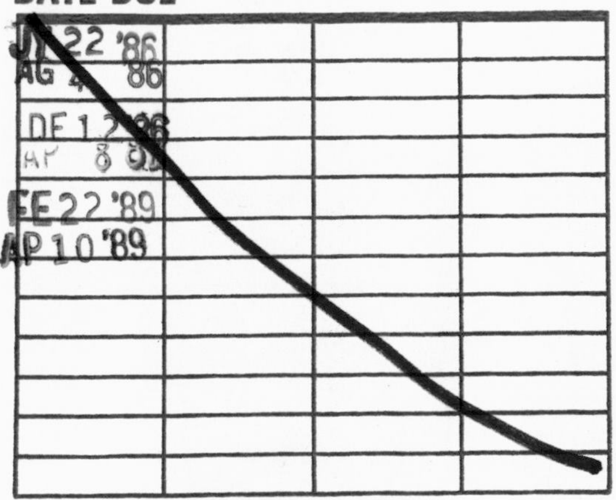

The Andrew R. Cecil Lectures on

Moral Values in a Free Society

established by

The University of Texas at Dallas

Volume II

THE ETHICS OF CITIZENSHIP

The Ethics of Citizenship

JAMES B. STOCKDALE
MARK O. HATFIELD
JOE H. FOY
ANDREW R. CECIL
LEON JAWORSKI

With an introduction by
ANDREW R. CECIL

The University of Texas at Dallas
1981

Printed in the United States of America
at The University of Texas at Dallas

Library of Congress Catalog Card Number: 81-50778

FOREWORD

In the brief twelve years since The University of Texas at Dallas was founded, a number of achievements have been recorded. Among those has been the establishment of the *Andrew R. Cecil Lectures on Moral Values in a Free Society.*

This series was named for Dr. Cecil, a Distinguished Scholar in Residence at the university and Chancellor of the Southwestern Legal Foundation. Throughout his career, Dr. Cecil has addressed the central moral values of his time, always stressing a faith in the dignity and worth of every individual, and we have focused the Cecil lectures so as to cast light on those principles and their importance to our nation.

We intend the selections to be a continuing part of the life of The University of Texas at Dallas, in service to our students as well as to the general public. As I noted in last year's series, the United States can point with justifiable pride to its achievements in many quarters—in the unparalleled freedom and well-being of its citizens and its progress in education, industry, the arts, science, and technology. Yet, these achievements are the heritage of the values instilled in our institutions and our traditions by our forefathers. One of the foremost duties of a university is to cast light on this heritage to ensure that it is understood and cherished and preserved.

The University of Texas at Dallas was greatly honored in 1980 by the participation of the five illustrious scholars who provided two days of insight and inspiration for our students and for area citizens. The success of that series is attributable to the superb papers of Messrs.

Andrew Cecil, Joe Foy, Mark Hatfield, Leon Jaworski, and James Stockdale which are presented here.

This, the second volume of proceedings of our series, is the direct result of the special generosity of those corporations, foundations, and individuals who have founded and are supporting this singularly important annual lecture series. We are most grateful to these enablers.

I hope that *The Ethics of Citizenship* will serve you as a benchmark of contemporary thought on the questions which face us today.

BRYCE JORDAN, President
The University of Texas at Dallas

December, 1980
Dallas, Texas

CONTENTS

Introduction 13
Andrew R. Cecil

Education for Leadership and Survival:
The Role of the Pressure Cooker 25
James B. Stockdale

Moral Majority or Servant Minority 55
Mark O. Hatfield

Moral Values in Business-Government Relations 75
Joe H. Foy

Education for Citizenship 99
Andrew R. Cecil

Ethics in Government 137
Leon Jaworski

INTRODUCTION

by

Andrew R. Cecil

One of the principal concerns of twentieth-century historians has been human progress. In his *A Study of History,* Arnold Toynbee tried to determine the reasons that lay behind the cyclical ups and downs of civilization, and found a pattern of symptoms of civilization in decay. Some of these symptoms are sadly in evidence today. Among these, too numerous to list, Toynbee's examples include the deterioration of the economy in both devaluation of currency and inflation, the end of citizen military service and the development of a voluntary professional army, increasing dependence on public funds and control, and decay in moral principles.

Among those who look to the cultures of Greece and Rome for chief inspiration, the British classicist Michael Grant, in his *The Fall of the Roman Empire—A Reappraisal* (The Annenberg School Press, Radnor, Pa., 1976), identifies in the contemporary society of the West the internal flaws which caused the fall of Rome by the degradation of values, the erosion of institutions, and the creation of a vacuum in the moral order that ought to unify a nation. He sees disunity as the primary cause of the fall of Rome. Among the problems he notes are the large gulf between social classes, the failure of the government and the people to communicate with and trust one another, the breakdown of alliances between nations, and complacency on the part of the citizens.

According to Grant, this process of decay is presently being repeated in the civilizations of Europe and the United States. Unless it is reversed, it will bring the West before long to the point that preceded the crumbling of Rome's walls in the fifth century.

No less revealing are the thoughts of Professor Robert Nisbet in his book *Twilight of Authority* (Oxford University Press, New York, 1975). In the two and a half millenia of Western history a number of major twilight ages have occurred, when authority was undermined and chaos approached. Professor Nisbet, in his belief that the twentieth century is a twilight age for the West, is "seeking to light up the present, chiefly the American present, in the historical perspective of twilight." He is concerned about the "social equalitarianism which is bred less by the moral value of equality than by centralized power's leveling effects upon the natural hierarchies of all social institutions" (p. vi). He is also disturbed by the continued trend toward "a military Leviathan," by the progressive inflation of values in all spheres, including the economic, and by the constantly increasing centralization of power.

Decline in popular trust of government and its leaders, loss of respect for law and the decline of forms in all spheres of social and political life, the growing conflict between democracy and bureaucracy, the specter of insecurity caused by the rising volume of crime and the increasing threat of terror, the diminishing ties of race, loyalty, religion, and kinship, the erosion of patriotism and of the sacred in human affairs, disillusionment in state and social order, and the dislocation of the local community are, according to Nisbet, some of the marks of the age in which we live, the age of crumbling social and cultural walls that have protected the Constitution and democracy. Professor Nisbet, in his concluding chapter on "The Restoration of Authority," wonders whether it is possible to arrest or reverse the "present accelerating tendencies toward political Leviathan on the one hand and moribundity of the social order on the other" (p. 230).

Many share the belief that today our civilization and our nation face the most serious crisis of the century, perhaps of many centuries, and are highly skeptical that the arrest or reversal of the social disintegration around us is possible. We dispute this idea, since we believe that the people of the United States of America are the heirs of a mighty heritage that bears within itself the power to confront and reduce the peril of any such crisis. George Santayana said that "To be an American is of itself almost a moral condition, an education, and a career." Each symptom of a decline in society creates a challenge that should bring forth the best efforts of the society to overcome the danger of decay.

Although the history of the United States demonstrates devotion to liberty, justice, and equality under the law, it cannot be denied that we also face an abundance of dilemmas. The responsibility for finding a balance between freedom and order, between the safety of our nation and the rights of the individual, and between the public and private interests is not limited to the three branches of our government, but should be shared by all citizens.

The decay of a civilization is not an inevitable disease which cannot be prevented; it does not come as a violent shock, like an earthquake. It can be counteracted, because changes in our society are not decreed by nature.

When symptoms of disorder appear, there is no reason to despair. Modern society has the ability to shape its destiny. Thomas Jefferson asserted that "morality, compassion, generosity are innate elements of the human condition." Since the behavior of society is the sum of the behavior of its members—its citizens—it is up to these citizens to understand and preserve the conditions which secure individual freedom and equal opportunity for all men, as well as responsible government under the rule of law.

History teaches us that the decay of various civilizations was caused not by the iron law of fate, but rather resulted from human failures to establish such values as constant concern for individual self-realization, respect for the dignity and worth of one's fellowman, and appreciation of the imperatives of social justice. It is, therefore, up to us as citizens to build a national community with a common moral language, which does not guarantee the elimination of evil but does assure the awareness of values which elevate and do not degrade.

Admiral James B. Stockdale's contribution to the present series of lectures vividly reminds us of the necessity of a system of moral awareness in a period of stress and hardship. He emphasizes not only the duties of citizenship, but the need to educate citizens by means of both the rigors of practical experience and the discipline of moral philosophy. His thesis is that the two go hand in hand—that the moral philosophy which has survived throughout the centuries was formed through exposure to the hard realities of life and that only armed with such lofty ideals as philosophy provides can man struggle with these realities and survive with honor and dignity. His touchstones for these ideals he locates not only in in the Judaeo-Christian tradition but also in the philosophical tradition that descends from the Greeks.

A citizen is a social as well as a political being. He needs government, but he also needs adequate controls to prevent the government from turning against him instead of serving him. This century has witnessed an extraordinary growth in government functions and a concommitant increase in the number and size of administrative agencies in response to the progressive extension of governmental responsibility, especially in the fields of economic regulations and public welfare. The emphasis on the importance of the general welfare does not mean that the state can always better promote social progress than could a system of private enterprise with limited governmental control. There is always the possibility that political power can become an instrument of exploitation through force, coercion, and other outrages against human personality. Similarly, overgrown individualism striving only for personal gain can result in injustice, since the interest of the few can be exercised to the disadvantage of the many.

The balance between the spheres of the public sector and the private sector is the topic of Mr. Joe. H. Foy's lecture in the 1980 series. Mr. Foy's argument is that on the whole, the balance between government and business in this country has been fair and productive. In an ideal world, there would be no need for laws or regulations of any sort, but in the world in which we live, that need does exist. In the analysis of the complex nature of ethics and business power, two ideas stand out in Mr. Foy's lecture: that insofar as leaders in the private sector accept the ethical postulates of service to their fellowman, they avoid the need for governmental control; and that a heightened sense of business ethics would contribute greatly to the common order and the welfare of our nation.

Mr. Foy's careful discrimination between private morality and public ethics and his insistence on the individual's responsibility remind us that in order for the individual to remain the master and not the slave of his political and social environment he must always be aware of the fragility of our institutions. As the history of the twentieth century has so painfully evidenced, democracy itself is the most delicate of institutions. There is a perennial need for careful watchfulness over it. If citizens are to satisfy in dignity their spiritual and material aspirations, they must strive for an ethical government in this seemingly unethical world. This they may do by taking part in the political process and by assuming the responsibilities of citizenship. One of these responsibilities is a concern for moral values and the recognition of the power of the individual conscience.

The ancient Egyptians and Jews did not have an articulated concept of the individual conscience. The system of collective virtues, rewards, and punishment they saw as inherent in God's order. The Jews, only two or three centuries before Christ, and the Greek philosophers developed the idea of the individual conscience. The New Testament inherited this idea and amplified it by asserting the unique personality of each individual and the immortality of his soul. The Judaeo-Christian philosophy gave birth to the idea of inalienable rights, of the rule of a law that can be invoked against the state, and of the maxim that governmental authority must always be kept in check.

This maxim proclaims that a person is more than a

political pawn enjoying only the privileges bestowed on him by the state. This maxim also proclaims that in matters of conscience, there is a moral power higher than the state. The ideas of individual freedom and of the necessity for checks in governmental authority led to the establishment in the United States of a separation of the legislative, executive, and judicial branches of government, an harmonious arrangement with an accountability for the performance of our governmental agencies which is indispensable for democracy. This accountability protects all from the inroads of excessive political power and corruption.

Mr. Leon Jaworski's address on "Ethics in Government" in the 1980 lecture series emphasizes the need for such an accountability from all our elected officials. Mr. Jaworski decries not only the disquieting events of recent years, in which flagrant violations of the public trust have come to light, but also the underlying public apathy which paved the way for wrongdoing. He counsels a balanced approach to correcting abuses, recollecting that drastic remedies often inflict worse problems than those they were designed to cure. Above all, Mr. Jaworski cautions that due responsibility for one's own actions is the surest safeguard against wrongdoing.

The history of mankind is the history of the search for the best kind of government, and we are still embarked on that search. The different kinds of government which have been suggested over the years may have one thing in common: the desire to protect the individual from the lawless and arbitrary ruler. Confucius with his code of right conduct, Plato with his idea of justice as defined in *The Republic,* Aristotle with his concept of the mixed state as sketched in his *Politics,* Cicero in restating the doctrine of a natural law which calls for respect for every human being, John Locke with his concept of unalienable rights which so influenced the Founding Fathers of this country, the writers of the Constitution themselves—all of them tried to channel the principles of morality into the avenues of political life.

We must be careful of the means by which we try to accomplish this valuable end. Senator Mark Hatfield in his address, "Moral Majority or Servant Minority," stresses that in a time such as our own, when individuals sense a collapse in moral values, various forces may arise and attempt to fill the resulting vacuum. In a time of apathy and of a hunger for wholeness, it is tempting for citizens to listen to voices which provide simplistic answers in an easy dogmatism. There is a danger when those who claim to speak for the church, in offering simplistic answers to complicated questions, inject themselves into political life by dictating what constitutes absolute morality. Senator Hatfield draws attention to the parallel between our own time and that of the Weimar Republic in Germany, when the voices of moderation were silenced by the roaring of those on the extremes of the political spectrum. We must beware of letting such extreme views prevail. Dogmatism is the enemy of a true moral consciousness. We must take care not to put our trust either in the idol of a dictatorial church or in the idol of a state which has assumed too much power. The individual must choose for himself the values by which he will live; he remains the master of his moral duties and his moral obligations.

The growth of social unrest resulted from bestowing on the government the role of the custodian of the common good. "Big Government" offering "equality" and "wider distribution of wealth" carries with it the wave of totalitarianism. When the claims on government have grown out of control and the constantly growing groups of special interests have joined the clamor for funds, the time is ripe to strive for social stability by lowering expectations of government handouts. It is time to combine the concern for the rights of a citizen with a sober stocktaking about the citizen's duties and his moral obligations.

When swollen claims on society propel the nation from the already highly modified version of capitalism to a stringently regulated economy with conflicting interests of various groups pushing dangerously against each other, educational institutions cannot escape their responsibility to cast light on the fundamental values on which our nation is based. In response to this challenge, they must recognize the influence that has been a part of the fabric of American life from the earliest days.

George Washington in his Farewell Address stressed the tie between religion and morality when he said: "Religion and morality are indispensable supports . . . great Pillars of human happiness. . .[the] firmest props of the duties of men and citizens . . . And let us with caution indulge the supposition, that morality can be maintained without religion. Whatever may be conceded to the influence of refined education on minds of peculiar structure, reason and experience both forbid us to expect that national morality can prevail in exclusion of religious principle."

As I point out in my lecture on "Education for Citizenship," Supreme Courts in various states have taken the position that Christian morality is the ethical code furnishing "the purest system of morality, the firmest auxiliary, and only stable support of human laws." The Establishment Clause of the Constitution does not bar teaching *about* religion, not even in state-supported higher education. A liberal education cannot be complete without the intellectual exercise of finding answers to questions concerning ultimate moral values. Study of religions and of basic concepts of religious faith, as some scholars maintain, serves to "uplift" the moral thinking of the college student, thus preparing him to discharge his moral obligations as a citizen.

The 1980 Lectures on Moral Values in a Free Society point in a single direction. Each of them stresses that to win the global war of ideas and to remain free, we will have to win the battle for the mind and spirit. Each of them also stresses the necessity for a strong sense of individual responsibility and honor. Aristotle in his *Politics* issued the warning: "For man, when perfected, is the best of animals, but, when separated from law and justice, he is the worst of all; . . . Wherefore, if he have no virtue, he is the most unholy and the most savage of animals, and the most full of lust and gluttony. But justice is the bond of men in states, and the administration of justice, which is the determination of what is just, is the principle of order in political society."

If our public order—whether in the private or the public sector—is to function with harmonious strength, we must return to the eternal values on which this country was founded. Our educational institutions and our leaders have a grave duty to see that these values are discussed and imparted and to bring conscience to bear on issues faced by our society. The well-being of our nation depends upon the individual conduct of our citizens, and that conduct vitally depends upon our allegiance to lasting moral values revolving, according to Plato, about the good of the whole.

EDUCATION FOR LEADERSHIP AND SURVIVAL: THE ROLE OF THE PRESSURE COOKER

by

James B. Stockdale

Admiral James B. Stockdale

Vice Admiral Stockdale, until recently the fifteenth president of The Military College of South Carolina, graduated from the United States Naval Academy in 1946, from the U.S. Naval Test Pilot School in 1954, and from the graduate school of Stanford University in 1962. The first twenty of his thirty-six years of active military service were highlighted by his engineering test flying and classroom teaching at the Naval Air Test Center, Patuxent River, Maryland, and by his pre-eminence as a fighter pilot and air wing commander at sea aboard aircraft carriers. He had more flight time in the supersonic F–8 single seat fighter than any man in the world when he led the United States' initial strikes against North Vietnam from a carrier deck in the Tonkin Gulf in August 1964.

Shot down and captured over a year later during another tour in Vietnam, he was kept in solitary confinement for most of his seven and one-half years of imprisonment. Despite years of torture and restraint in leg irons and handcuffs, then-Captain Stockdale maintained contact with his fellow Americans by clandestine means, setting standards and policy for the prisoners' organization and united resistance.

Throughout three flag officer tours following the war, Admiral Stockdale placed ever-increasing emphasis on writing and teaching. As president of the Naval War College, he broke precedent by joining his faculty as a classroom instructor. He introduced the discipline of philosophy into that institution's graduate level curriculum, originating and teaching a course entitled "The Foundations of Moral Obligation."

Vice Admiral Stockdale holds six honorary doctoral degrees; his personal combat decorations include two Distinguished Flying Crosses, three Distinguished Service Medals, four Silver Stars, two Purple Hearts, and the Congressional Medal of Honor. He is president of his Naval Academy class, a member of MENSA, The Tavern Club of Boston, and The Explorers Club of New York.

EDUCATION FOR LEADERSHIP AND SURVIVAL: THE ROLE OF THE PRESSURE COOKER

by

Vice Admiral James B. Stockdale, U.S. Navy (Retired)

Chancellor Cecil's expressed wish is to center this lecture series around the theme of Citizenship and Moral Obligation. Taken generally, my subject—Education for Leadership and Survival—falls easily within this comprehensive category. My subtitle—The Role of the Pressure Cooker—projects an angle of vision that is scarcely less universal. Though it subtends a very personal arc, it points back to the Christian and classical past. I am all for the idea of progress, but I believe that all progress is stimulated by an awareness of a heritage. "It is the future that we are more likely to think of immediately when the idea of progress is brought up," says Robert Nisbet, "but it was only when men became conscious of a long past . . . that a consciousness of progressive movement from past to present became possible." (*History of the Idea of Progress*, New York, 1980, p. 323.)

Let me start with the over-obvious, boxed in a cliche, wrapped in some truisms. The concept of citizenship is one of the fundamental ideas of Western civilization. It is an idea born with the Greeks more than 2500 years ago. It is an idea fundamental to the American republic. It is an idea historically linked to two others: freedom and organization. At its highest, citizenship achieves a balance between these two elements necessary to the survival of society. At its best, citizenship finds an equilibrium between two essential ingredients—that of rights, and that of duties. When the idea of citizenship is losing its grip, one or the other of these elements becomes eroded. Either freedom is on the losing end, or the sense of duty, of obligation, goes down the drain. We are living at a time when the idea of citizenship has been seriously weakened. We have a strong sense of the rights of a citizen. But we've lost much of the sense of the corresponding duties and obligations of citizenship. Meanwhile, the State behaves in a paradoxical manner. We find ourselves in what the philosophers call a dialectical situation. Responding to popular demand for freedom and equality, the bureaucracy of the State, swollen to the proportions of a Titan, enacts battery after battery of laws and regulations to ensure that freedom and equality. Result: the State's liberty is impaired as is that of its citizens. Like a giant Gulliver the State lies on the ground, struggling to move against the bonds of the very measures it has taken to ensure freedom and equality. For "Freedom and equality are sworn enemies," say the Durants in their little book *The Lessons of History*, "and when one prevails the other dies." (New York, 1968, p. 20.) This is a hard saying. I will let you decide what measure of truth it has.

One of the primary duties of citizenship is its duty to education. By education I don't mean just schooling. The idea of education is broader than that, important though schooling is. Schooling is a necessary element of education, but not sufficient completely to define it.

Marriage and family life are education. Sport, play, and entertainment are education. Religious training is education. Friendship is education. Military service is education. Any and every encounter with nature and society is education. Some social scientists call education in this comprehensive sense "acculturation." I prefer to call it more simply—"experience."

Now there is an element in education that I consider of crucial importance. There are learned names for the many varieties of this element, and some of these we might talk about as we go on. But for the moment I'll use the word "stress." Another name for it is "pressure." Stress or pressure in education and in life has had bad reviews. I want to give it a good one. Doctors used to say stress was bad for you—one of the evils of competitive society—and should be avoided. Nowadays some doctors say a moderate amount of stress is good for you, particularly the kind that comes from physical exercise. And there's a whole school of Running Doctors like George Sheehan who get a kind of mystical experience from running a marathon and write books about it. (Cf. Sheehan, *Running and Being,* New York, 1978.) But all doctors say if you're planning to get into this, get a stress test first.

Stress is essential to leadership. Living with stress, knowing how to handle pressure, is necessary for survival. It is related to a man's ability to wrest control of his own destiny from the circumstances that surround him. Or, if you like, to prevail over technology. Tied up with this ability is something I can express in one word, "improvisation." I mean man's ability to prepare a response to a situation while under pressure.

George Bernard Shaw said that most people who fail complain that they are the victims of circumstances. Those who get on in this world, he said, are those who go out and look for the right circumstances. And if they can't find them they make their own.

To wrest or not to wrest control of one's destiny is a subject discussed by Will and Ariel Durant in that little book I mentioned. In the chapter of their *Lessons in History* called "Growth and Decay," they state that what determines whether the challenge of history will or will not be met depends upon "the presence or absence of creative individuals with a clarity of mind and energy of will (almost a definition of genius), capable of effective responses to new situations (almost a definition of intelligence)." I think the Durants' creative individual with energy of will, capable of effective responses to new situations, is the man I describe as one who can improvise under pressure.

My pitch is that if the energy of will and creativity necessary to improvise under pressure can be taught, they are best learned in a stressful regime—in a crucible of pressure, whether that crucible be a classroom or a total environment.

I suppose my coming down on the side of stress is no surprise to this audience. My life has been that of a military man, and pressure has been my constant companion. I began with a service academy education back in the time when every teacher had to register a grade for every student at every class meeting. That may not have been the best of all educational systems, but it was a stressful one. Afterward, I lived in stress for thirty years, as a fighter pilot, experimental test pilot, and prisoner of war. My last Navy assignment was the presidency of the Naval War College, where I taught a course "Foundations of Moral Obligation." Later I became president of a college which has for one hundred forty years educated young men in a stressful regime—The Citadel.

My lifetime of experience in the pressure cooker,

whether hemmed in by the iron laws of aerodynamics at 40,000 feet or on the flight test ranges over the Mojave Desert, or hemmed in by the iron laws of extortion in the prisons of Hanoi, has led me to conclude that once one learns to accommodate the shocks of a stressful existence, his adrenalin, will power, and imagination are going to start churning to provide the maximum performance of the human mind. The generation I taught at test pilot school at the Naval Air Test Center at Patuxent River, Maryland (John Glenn was one of my classmates), could have stepped right out of the pages of Tom Wolfe's recent book, *The Right Stuff.* In those days of the early 1950s, the exciting subject was supersonic flight. I taught an academic course in thrust and drag in the high subsonic and lower supersonic flight regimes, and I can honestly say that the intellectual mastery of the graphs and the physical laws behind them were more efficiently taught to my students in the stress of actual flight in a cockpit at 40,000 feet than in the classroom. By saying that, I am not just referring to the difference between the classroom and the lab, but rather to the more mentally stimulating of the two environments.

But I don't want you to think that I am holding up my experiences under stress as a simple model of education for excellence and survival. I'll tell you more about those experiences in a moment, but first I want to broaden the screen a bit lest you think that stress and pressure are tied in a beneficial way to one way of life alone, however important they may have been in that life, which happened to be the life of a military man subjected perhaps to more direct and dire pressures than most. I want you to see with me that our whole culture, even what we call Western civilization itself, is founded on the sufferings and greatness of human beings and human societies under pressure.

It is a commonplace to say that our moral heritage has two sources—Judaic and Greek. The source book of the one is the Bible and the tradition of Judeao-Christianity associated with it. The origins of the other lie in the library of poetry, drama, politics, and philosophy of the Greek writers whose works have come down to us. If you are going to talk about justice, you had better begin with Job and Socrates.

If ever a man was in a pressure situation, it is Job, the man from the land of Uz. He is a man, once prosperous and happy, who has been struck by terrible misfortune. He has at a stroke lost sons and daughters, servants and possessions. He has been infected with a loathsome disease. Once a rich man, he now sits on an ash heap, naked, scraping his flesh with potsherds. He asks, "Why me, O Lord?" For he believes that the Almighty has caused or allowed these calamities to come upon him, and it makes no sense. He, Job, is a good man, a just man. What has he done to deserve this evil? Job wants to talk to God about this. Is He not a just God?

Now, as we know, God does not answer Job in the terms he would like. God does not acknowledge Job's virtue nor does He admit the situation is unfair. Instead, clothed in a whirlwind, He points to the awesome dimensions of the universe and asks Job if he, finite creature, could do anything like that. Can Job create the sea, guide the courses of the stars? Where was Job when God created heaven and earth?

In answer, Job is silent. He bows and puts his hand over his mouth. His silence is the silence of faith, of endurance. Job was put under stress greater than nearly any man could take, and he stood the test.

Theologians have found many exalted lessons in the story of Job. One of them is that we should not try to measure the standards of the infinite with those of the finite—they are incommensurable. The lesson I take from Job is simpler. Life is not fair. There is no moral economy or balance in the nature of things such that virtue is rewarded and vice punished. The good man hangs on and hangs in there. It is significant that the nearest Plato comes to a definition of courage in the dialogue *Laches* where Socrates is talking to a general under whom he served is "Courage is endurance of the soul." The Greeks admired the bold stroke, the audacious dash, but reserved top credit for the man that holds on under pressure. They knew by bitter experience what stress situations are. They knew what it means to break under pressure and what it means to hold on. On the battlefield, says Aristotle, the greatest pressure is fear of death, and the temptation is to run away. But the courageous man holds on.

Plato's dialogues' most compelling portraits of Socrates show his master handling himself under supreme stress. Defending himself on a capital charge in court before hostile judges, he resists their pressure to get himself off the hook by agreeing to renounce teaching and inquiry. In prison, he resists pressure to escape laid on him by his rich pupil Crito who had the means and the bribe money. (Athenians, "children of the laws," were not to be disillusioned by his failure to abide by the state's verdict, even though unjust.) With death only hours away he has the equanimity to advise his family and to discourse to his pupils on the Soul—on the reasons why a good man should not fear death. (*Apology* 29-30; *Crito* 50-51;

Phaedo 67-68.)

The Greek city-state itself was a bit like a pressure cooker. It was small, and life was pretty constricted within it. The pressure set up jealousies and envies, both internal and external; this was one reason why these political entities were always fighting with one another and exiling or deposing their own leaders. The Greek city-state was always in danger of being attacked by its neighbor. This was why military training was so much a part of the Greek citizen's life. It is true that some city-states at certain times used mercenaries or hired armies. But in general the latter were considered inferior and untrustworthy when the going got tough. The citizen army was at the heart of Greek city-state defense. Socrates did his military service in the Peloponnesian War, saw action at Potidaea and the siege of Delium, and passed up a decoration for valor so that another man might have it.

Education in ancient Greece came down hard on physical training. This training had an esthetic purpose. A body in good shape was fair to look upon. More than that, Greek gymnastics aimed at victory—victory in war and in the competitive games of peace. Greek gymnastic exercise was advantageous for military proficiency. One of the famous Spartan exercises was dancing—in heavy armor. This helped to develop the agility a man needed to wield off his offensive weapons, the spear and short sword; it also developed the finesse to sidestep the thrusts of his enemy. The philosopher Alfred North Whitehead, while teaching at Harvard, said that if Plato were to come to our country today, he would first ask to meet, not a philosopher, but a championship-class boxer.

In times of peace—and there were few—there were the

competitions among the city-states. The Olympic games, though only one of several periodic competitions, were the most famous of these contests. In fact, these games were so important to the Greeks that they suspended hostilities, if at war, for the duration. Today some educators talk about the evil effects of competition instilled into our children, of the need to avoid developing a competitive spirit in our youth. But the Greeks, whose humanism these same experts profess to admire, were the most competitive people that ever lived. They wanted to excel in everything. Their motto was *ai en aristeuein*, "always to be the best." Their public games included competition not only in racing, jumping, javelin throwing, boxing, and wrestling, but also in musical, poetic, literary, and drama contests. In one of the best known and most fun-filled dialogues of Plato, *The Symposium*, the party scene is the celebration of the prize the host Agathon had just won for writing the best tragedy. To the Greeks the heart of the game was *agon*—competition, stress, pressure, struggle to win. (Later we'll see a contemporary scholar's comment on *agon* in education.) They like to point out that the philosopher Heraclitus, to them already an ancient and legendary figure, had claimed that both music and science had their beginning in stress—the world itself composed of opposite forces, tensions pulling against each other, like the strain of a drawn bow, resulting in a comparative stability or permanence—as the strings of a lyre give forth harmony when they are pulled two ways, stretched in harmonic proportions over the sounding board of the instrument by the pegs and the tailboard fastenings. The beautiful repose of the Greek temple was seen by the intelligentsia as the product of perfectly calculated architectural stress.

Far more ancient than the dialogues of Plato or even the philosophy of Heraclitus is Homer's great story of Odysseus, soldier and navigator. In the *Odyssey* we read of his long captivity under Calypso and his twelve-year voyage, fraught with a score of deadly perils, from that rocky island where he was held enslaved, to Ithaca, where his faithful wife Penelope and his son Telemachus were waiting for him. We all know Homer's trick of tagging things, men and gods, with a characteristic label. It is always the wine-dark sea, always the grey-eyed Athena, always the rosy-fingered dawn. Odysseus' characteristic trait is resourcefulness, the ability to improvise in a pressure situation. *Polumetis*, Homer calls him, full of survival tricks, never at a loss no matter how lethal the situation may be. A familiar episode in the story illustrates Odysseus' resourcefulness under stress. Held captive by the one-eyed giant Polyphemus, in his narrow cave, Odysseus knows that he and his men are doomed to a horrible death. (That's a fair amount of pressure. Doctor Johnson told Boswell that when a man knows he's going to be hanged in a month, it concentrates his mind wonderfully.) Odysseus had only a couple of days. He waited until the giant was in a drunken sleep, then took a stake he had hidden in straw, heated it and plunged it into his captor's one eye, blinding him so that the Trojan war veteran and what was left of his crew could escape. Odysseus, the resourceful, kept his head; he had the ability to improvise under pressure.

A more profoundly moving story lies at the base and heart of Christianity itself—the death of Jesus on the Cross. By comparison, Socrates' death was merciful and dignified. Death by crucifixion was very cruel. Reserved for slaves and the most ignominious of criminals, this mode of execution killed by weakening the chest muscles by the downward drag of the body so that life was slowly extinguished by gradual and painful suffocation. What the stress was upon that man who hung there is hard for us to imagine—maybe not quite so hard for those of us who have experienced physical torture. The Gospel story tells us that despite the pressure to defend Himself at His trial, Jesus did not do so. On the cross, He kept silent in the face of his tormentors' jokes. He did cry out, "I thirst," and, when the anguish became more than a man could bear, "My God, My God, why hast Thou forsaken me?" But at the end He said as one would speak of a duty discharged, a mission completed, "It is finished."

Ernest Hemingway, hardly a model Christian, wrote a story called "Good Friday." It is a story about the aftermath of Calvary. Some Roman soldiers who were in charge of the execution are drinking and talking of the events of the day. They are pretty drunk. One soldier can only mumble over and over, "I tell you, He looked pretty good in there today." No accident that Hemingway's moral ideal was "grace under pressure." He tried to see that his heroes measured up to it.

In the Christian Middle Ages, especially as they were drawing to their close, alchemy was all the rage among a certain class of learned men. Alchemy was based on the old idea of the *hermetic* that had come down from ancient Greece and Egypt and had been colored by Christian sacramental teaching. The idea of the hermetic was twofold. It meant something sealed off—hermetically sealed, as we say. And it also meant magic—particularly magical transformation. You put something in a crucible or a retort and you subjected it to certain pressures like heat, or doses of sulphur and mercury. If you were lucky or wise or both, some kind of creative transformation would take place. In physical terms, this referred to the changing of base metals into precious ones—lead into gold. But the top grade alchemical philosophers were not content with mere physical crucibles and crystal retorts you could hold in your hand. They were aiming at even more important things. Paracelsus thought it might be possible to create a human being (homunculus) in the laboratory—something today people are again getting uneasy about. The higher alchemy aimed not at mere physical change but at moral and spiritual transformation. The crucible and retort became symbols of creative growth. Fire and the twin elements, sulfur and mercury, came to represent the outside pressures exerted upon the human soul in its confined place. In extreme cases, the fire might be of hellish origin. But if the soul in question were strong enough, inventive enough, not mere passive matter, that spirit might undergo an alchemical change—a metamorphosis of the spirit in which the ordinary stuff of humanity could turn into something precious, emerging as if from a tightly sealed cocoon.

This alchemy comparison may seem farfetched, but I find it not a bad fit with the experience several of us Americans had as long-term prisoners of the North Vietnamese in the dungeons of Hanoi. (I personally was there for nearly eight years, more than half of that time under the extreme discipline of torture and solitary confinement.) I think I know now what the old alchemists meant when they said that sometimes it took a little hell-fire to effect the magical transformation in the crucible. A prison is the most merciless case of sealing off a human soul in a confined space. For most people it is a degrading experience. It was for me too, but something more. In that tiny space of confinement, sealed off not only from the rest of the world but even from my fellow prisoners and comrades, I had an humble experience of moral and spiritual enlightenment. Although I am no match for certain great men of history, I find I had precedent and noble company.

The prison where Socrates awaited execution in Athens in the year 399 B.C. was not a marble columned palace as some of the Italian Renaissance masters painted it. Probably it was no more than a fair-sized cave in a hillside with iron bars across the opening. Here Socrates gave his last discourse to his students, many of whom wept, Plato tells us, as they listened to the master's words. He told them that we should not fear death, for death is the liberation of the soul from the body. During life, the soul lives in the body as if it were a prisoner, a caged bird. With death, the prison door is opened, the bird is set free. Socrates quotes a line from the old Orphic priests who said that the body is a tomb of the soul, the place of corruption. But the place of corruption is also the place of rebirth, of resurrection, freeing the spirit to take its rightful place in the divine realm from which it came. So the wise man does not fear death. It is not an evil. No harm can befall a good man.

In Italy, in the early centuries of Christian Rome, a man named Boethius was imprisoned by his emperor Theodoric the Ostrogoth. He was executed on a charge of treason in the year 524 A.D. This man Boethius was both a statesman and a scholar. He had been prime minister to the emperor. His scholarly works would have an immense influence on subsequent medieval philosophy. His commentaries on Aristotle's logic became standard texts in the universities. According to Boethius' written description of his imprisonment, he sits there in captivity lamenting his misfortune, the loss of his honors and riches, the confiscation of his library with bookshelves of glass and ivory. Suddenly a beautiful lady appears to him. She is Lady Philosophy. She comforts him by telling him many things. That the world is governed by divine wisdom, not by blind chance. That we must not give too much importance to Fortune, for she is a fickle lady, taking away with one hand what she has given with the other. We must not become upset when she takes good things away from us. They were never ours to begin with. True happiness does not come from externals, she reminds him, but from within. True, life with its sudden falls of fortune is no easy thing. But would a good soldier fighting a tough battle stop to say to himself how unhappy he is? A wise man like Boethius ought not to bewail his struggles with fortune any more than a brave soldier should be scared by the noises of battle. Lady Philosophy reminds the prisoner of the wisdom of Socrates—that no evil can befall a good man.

Boethius wrote his book while in prison. It was published after his death, and became one of the great Christian classics—*The Consolation of Philosophy.*

About 400 years ago a Spanish officer lay in prison, a captive of the Moors of Algeria. He was a veteran of the battle of Lepanto, the last great naval fight in which ships were powered by oars. The Turks had been encroaching on the Mediterranean with the aim of seizing Cyprus from Venice. But Don John of Austria, leading the ships of Spain and the Venetian Republic, destroyed the Turkish fleet in a fierce engagement from which this

Spanish officer emerged a cripple. He got no glory out of it for he was soon captured by Algerian pirates and held captive for five years with several of his comrades. At first he was profoundly depressed in his captivity, but gradually discovered in himself the power of leadership, the ability to organize and to direct men. He kept his comrades busy with tasks that took their minds off their sorry condition. He organized six elaborate escape attempts, all of which failed. At last he was released and returned to his native land of Spain where he expected the king to recognize his services. But the king and people were tired of wars and battles; they wanted to hear no more about it. Embittered, the officer withdrew to his home and began to scribble a comic story about a witless Don who fancied himself a knight errant of old and rode all over Spain seeking to conquer giants and rescue damsels in distress. The story grew under the fingers of his one good hand, and at last it was published under the title *Don Quixote.* The officer's name was Miguel de Cervantes.

The Stoic philosopher Epictetus was foremost among my consolations of philosophy in the pressure cooker of Hanoi. Like Cervantes he was a cripple. Unlike the author of *Don Quixote,* he was a slave. At least, he had been a slave until a generous master set him free so that he could teach philosophy in ancient Rome. How I got to know Epictetus I explained in a letter I wrote in 1975 to Joseph Brennan, then Professor of Philosophy, Barnard College, Columbia University, who had written to me asking about the comfort and strength philosophical readings had given me throughout my eight years in prison. I expanded these thoughts and added to them later in an article I wrote for *The Atlantic Monthly* titled

"The World of Epictetus" (April 1978). For what follows I'll draw on the letter. (The full text is in J.G. Brennan, *The Education of a Prejudiced Man*, New York, 1977. See also his "Hermetically Sealed" in *Perspectives and Personalities, Essays in Honor of Claude Hill*, Heidelberg, 1978.)

I came into the Navy as a Naval Academy Midshipman in 1943 at the age of 19. For the next twenty years or so I was a rather technically oriented person. I was a seagoing destroyer officer, an aviator, a landing signal officer, a test pilot and academic instructor at the test pilot school, a many-times-deployed fighter pilot, and ultimately a Squadron Commander of a supersonic F-8 Crusader outfit.

In 1960 I was sent to Stanford University for two full years' study in politics/history/economics in preparation for later assignments in politico-military policymaking. I loved the subject matter, but noticed that in many courses my interest would peak at about the time the professor would say, "We're getting into philosophy—let's get back to the subject." I had more than adequate time to get the expected Master's Degree, and suggested to my advisor in my second year that I sign up for some courses over in the philosophy corner of the quadrangle. He was dead set against it—thought it would be a waste of my time. He said, "That's a very technical subject—it would take two terms to learn their peculiar vocabulary." Finally, after I persisted, he said, "It's up to you."

It was my good fortune on that first morning that I wandered through the halls of the Philosophy Department, grey-haired and in civilian clothes, to come by an open office whose occupant asked if he could be of help. When I told him that I was a graduate student technically in the humanities but with no formal philosophy background, he could scarcely believe it. When I told him I was a naval officer, he asked me to have a seat. He had been in the Navy in World War II. His name was Philip Rhinelander. As a Harvard lawyer he had practiced in Boston for several years before Pearl Harbor, volunteered for war service at sea, and thereafter took his PhD at Harvard. After tours as a dean at Harvard he was back in the classroom at his own request. He was in the midst of his two-term "personal" course: "The Problems of Good and Evil." This he had built upon the lessons of the Book of Job ("Life is not fair"). He offered to let me enter the course, and to overcome my shortcomings of background, to give me an hour of private tutoring each week. What a departure from other departments! (In some, PhD candidates sat outside their advisor's office for hours on end awaiting a ten-minute conversation.) I loved Rhinelander's class, and particularly our hour together each week. I remember how patient he was in trying to get me to realize the full implications of Hume's "Dialogues on Natural Religion."

As we parted after our last session, he reached up to his bookshelf and said something like, "As I remember it, you are a military man—take this booklet as a memento of our hours together. It provides moral philosophy applicable to your profession." It was Epictetus' *Enchiridion.*

That night I started to peruse my gift. I recognized nothing that applied to the career I had known. I was a fighter pilot, an organizer, a motivator of young aviators, a martini drinker, a golf player, a technologist—and this ancient rag talked about not concerning oneself with matters over which one had no control, etc. Charitably put, I thought it irrelevant. Nevertheless I read and remembered almost all of it—if for no other reason than that it was given to me by a man I respected as a human being, a scholar, and a teacher.

About three years after I had said good-bye to Rhinelander, while in the midst of my second combat tour against North Vietnam as a Wing Commander, I pulled off a target one September morning in the midst of heavy flak when all the lights came on (fire warning, hydraulic failure, electrical failure, etc.). As I sped over the treetops it became immediately apparent that I had lost my flight controls—by reflex action I pulled the curtain and ejected—and was almost immediately suspended in the air 200 feet above a village street, in total silence except for rifle shots and the whir of bullets past my ear. So help me, in those fleeting seconds before I landed among the waiting crowd I had two vivid thoughts: (1) Five years to wait (I had studied enough modern Far East history and talked to enough Forward Air Controllers in the south to appreciate fully the dilemma of Vietnam—I turned out to be an optimist by two and one-half years), and (2) I am leaving that technological world and entering the world of Epictetus.

The world view of the Stoics, Professor Rhinelander had joked, was that their environment was a buzz saw in which human *will* was the only salvation. I was to spend over four years combating a veritable buzz saw (until the torture and extortion machine was set in idle in the late autumn of 1969) and over three more years of simple deprived detention of the sort one would expect in a primitive hostile country. All told, four years were to be spent in solitary confinement, nearly half of it in leg irons. Throughout, until 1970, every effort was to be made to break my will, to make me a cat's paw in propaganda schemes. Real or fabricated "violations of the established regulations for criminals' detention" (*e.g.*, tapping on the walls to another prisoner) would result in torture, with the end aim of sequential (1) confession of guilt, (2) begging for forgiveness, (3) apology, and (4) atonement (signing an antiwar statement). A similar sequence would be set up with *particular* gusto if I were found to be exercising leadership of others via the tap code ("inciting other criminals to oppose the camp authority").

The stress situation was thus framed in the above context. I was crippled (knee broken, partial use of arm); alone; sick (weight down 50 pounds); depressed (not so much from anticipating the next pain as from the prospect of my eventually losing my honor and self-respect); and helpless except for will. What conditions could be more appropriate for Epictetus' admonitions? As a soldier, I had bound myself to a military ethic:

> Remember that you are an actor in a drama of such sort as the author chooses—if short, then in a short one: if long, then in a long one. If it be his pleasure that you should enact a poor man, see that you act it well; or a cripple, or a ruler, or a private citizen. For this is your business—to act well the given part; but to choose it belongs to another.

I was crippled:

> Sickness is an impediment to the body, but not to the will unless itself pleases. Lameness is an impediment to the leg, but not to the will; and say this to yourself with regard to everything that happens. For you will find it to be an impediment to something else, but not truly to yourself.

I was dependent on my extortionists for life support, and soon learned to ask for nothing to avoid demands for "reciprocity":

> Whoever then would be free, let him wish nothing, let him decline nothing, which depends on others; else he must necessarily be a slave.

I could stop misery at any time by becoming a puppet; was it worth the shame?

> If some person had delivered up your body to some passer-by, you would certainly be angry. And do you feel no shame in delivering up your own mind to any reviler, to be disconcerted and confounded?

Relief from boils, heat, cold, broken bones was "available" for the asking—for a price. What should I say?

> If I can get them with the preservation of my own honor and fidelity and self-respect, show me the way and I will get them; but if you require me to lose my own proper good, that you may gain what is no good, consider how unreasonable and foolish you are. (*Enchiridion*, XVII, IX, XIV, XXVII, XXIV.)

Epictetus was not the only valuable philosophic memory in my predicament: Job (Why me . . . Why *not* me?), Descartes' bifurcation of mind and body, and many other readings were invaluable. Some of my prison mates had deep religious convictions which served them well, some drew resolve from their concepts of political virtue, and so on in a broad spectrum of varying levels of sophistication. I thought of God, and I thought of country too, and that helped. But my "secret weapon" was the security I felt in anchoring my resolve to those selected portions of philosophic thought that emphasized human dignity and self-respect. Imprisonment under dire stress was for me, as it has been for certain others, the crucible in which an ordinary man was made to realize that there was something in him that under pressure could transcend the ordinary. In that hermetic closed space, sealed off from human contact, subjected to pressures of outward forces that reached into the soul, I experienced my own illumination. I would never be the same again. Jack Kerouac, King of the Beats, is not my kind of man, but I am with him when he says "Prison is where you promise yourself the right to live."

Prison is not the only sealed-off place in which development of the spirit under pressure may occur. Any ship is a cutoff world under stress, and it is no accident that our greatest American novel, Melville's *Moby Dick*, rose from the close confinement of its author in a succession of whaling and naval vessels that did not bring him back to these shores for three years. The cockpit of the plane, the command center, the chess board, the sports arena—these and other closed spaces can be the scene of creative transformation of self. In science there is the laboratory, its test tubes and crucibles; in religion, the ark and the tabernacle. I need not mention that the miraculous development of human life itself takes place in the sealed-off space of the womb.

I am not claiming that we should base education on training people to be in prison, but I am saying that in stress situations, the fundamentals, the hard-core classical subjects, are what serve best. I'm not the only prisoner who discovered that so-called practical academic exercises in "how to do things" were useless in that fix. The classics have a way of saving you the trouble of prolonged experiences. You don't have to go out and buy pop psychology self-help books. When you read the classics in the humanities, you become aware that the big ideas have been around a long time, despite the fact that they are often served up today in modern psychological "explanations" of human action as novel and "scientific." We didn't have to wait for Horney, Erikson, and Maslow to give us the notion of self-fulfillment or self-actualization. They were there in Aristotle's treatises on psychology and ethics all along. Of course, modern psychotherapists have to touch them up a bit to bring them up to date, by injecting a heady dose of personal individualism. This would have puzzled Aristotle. He would not have understood what good it does to discover "the real Me." He thought that self-realization could not be achieved without service to the community, in his case, the city-state. His time was not what Tom Wolfe calls a "Me" generation.

Can we educate for leadership? That's a tough question. It's related to—it's really a part of—a similar question: Can moral values, can moral excellence be taught? There's a great deal of concern about that today. We hear that we must get back to teaching moral values to the young. But can they be taught? Socrates raised the question in the *Meno,* and declined to give a straight answer. His pitch went something like this. It seems that moral values can't be taught, for if they could, why is it that fine men like Pericles, who have given their children the best home environment and schooling, have no-good sons? It seems that "up to the present at least," he said, moral excellence must be considered as something we are endowed with, a gift from the gods, like personal beauty or blue eyes and curly hair. But that "up to the present" is important. Socrates does not close the door entirely on the question. Maybe if we could work out a science of the good, in which a model state based on justice will help us understand how to educate for the good, we might just do it, we might just be able to teach something about moral excellence and make it stick. So Plato follows the *Meno* with the *Republic*, in which he constructs just such a model state in which each is given his or her due. I say "her" advisedly because women as well as men will receive top education in Plato's ideal city-state. And as a military man I'm glad to know that Plato reserves a high status and important function for graduates of his equivalent of West Point and Annapolis.

Aristotle has a lot of common sense to offer on this question of the teaching of moral excellence and leadership. His answer to the question has been taken up into the Western tradition, modified by Locke in the 17th century and by Rousseau in the 18th, then shaped by our own founding fathers, particularly by Thomas Jefferson, author of our Declaration of Independence. We are not born good, but we naturally are adapted to become so. And this adaptation means building of character by habit and training on a basis of free choice. "Neither by nature nor contrary to nature do the moral excellences arise in us," Aristotle says, "rather we are adapted by nature to receive them, and made perfect by habit." (*Nichomachean Ethics*, 1103a 24-26.)

Aristotle was much interested in the role of stress and pressure in life situations, because of his profound concern with the distinction between actions which are performed in force-situations and those freely chosen. There are some actions in which the agent plays no part, he says, and gives the examples of hostages taken prisoner and a man tied up so that he cannot move. A true human act is one in which intention and free choice are present.

But he was especially interested in situations in which compulsion and choice can coexist. Even though I may be a prisoner or a hostage, some measure of freedom remains to me. In our situation in Hanoi we were helplessly *confined* and at the mercy of the enemy. Yet a crucial measure of freedom remained to us. We could collaborate with the enemy or could refuse to do so. True, he had the power to make us confess to shameful things by torture. (The method was simple—arms tied behind the back and the rope progressively tightened as blood circulation was stopped until the strongest man would scream in pain like a baby.) But we still had the power to make him begin all over again the next day. Time and again one of our men would come back from interrogation ashamed because he had given up information under torture. By the tap code we'd tell him that we had done that and worse. "There are some instances," says Aristotle, "when a man acts improperly under a strain greater than human nature can bear and which no one could endure." But he adds, "Yet there are perhaps also acts which no man could possibly be compelled to do, but rather than do them he would accept the most terrible suffering and death." (*Nichomachean Ethics,* III, 1110a 23-28.) In Hanoi I realized that my captors had all the power. I couldn't see how I was going to keep my honor and self-respect intact. The one thing I held on to was my knowing that if you don't give up, compromise, and literally "spill your guts," you can't be had. Compromises pile up when you're in a pressure situation in the hands of a skilled extortionist. You can be had if you make that first compromise, offer to make that "deal," or "meet them half way."

It may seem strange for someone with a deep commitment to the humanities in education to defend the old Plebe Year practices at Annapolis, the U.S. Naval Academy. That's a rough year. The midshipman is studying under great pressure, and he is constantly subjected to personal stresses that some might think of as pointless harassment. But that year of education under stress was of great personal survival value to me. I recall about a month after I was back from Vietnam one of my former prison mates came running to me after a reunion at the Naval Academy. He told me with glee, "This is really great, you won't believe how this country has advanced. They've practically done away with the Plebe Year at the Academy and they've got computers in the basement of Bancroft Hall." I thought, "Hell, if there was anything that helped us get through those eight years it was Plebe Year, and if anything screwed up that war, it was computers."

To me the greatest educational fallacy is that you can get it without stress. The student revolts in the colleges and universities of the 1960s forced faculty and administrators to back down, to take away requirements, to call off pressures, make things easy. No more required hard science. No more required foreign languages. "Take-home tests" and cozy chats took the place of rigorous final examinations. Students were allowed to take what they wanted. What they wanted was social science, urban development, psychology. What they didn't want was history, mathematics, physics, formal logic, classics, and modern foreign languages. Any reform demanded and secured was always in the direction of easing pressure, lowering standards, diminishing rigor—never increasing it. Result? More than a decade of poorly educated young men and women. In response to the economic pressures of the 1970s, the faculty knuckle-under process has begun to turn around. But it will take a lot of turning before education gets back on the rails.

There is a fascinating essay by Dr. Walter Ong in *Daedalus* magazine, titled “Agonistic Structures in Academia.” (*Daedalus*, Fall 1974, No. 4.) His purpose is to offer background material that would help educators analyze the campus struggles of the 1960s. One of the most important factors involved, says Ong, is the disappearance of a stabilizing stressful enmity that for 1600 years had pitted students against teachers in ceremonial combat. Ong quotes an old German who in the late 1960s was teaching in a public high school in New York. After a trying day in class, he was heard to exclaim, “Ach, these boys want me to be their friend; they should know that the teacher should always be their enemy.”

Until recent decades, ceremonial combat in the educational process had been part of Western culture. The student-teacher face-off had been standard since the early stages of the Christian era. Saint Augustine described the stand-off methodology in his *Confessions*. Dialectic was the struggle of opposites, and dialectic was the standard method of education in the universities of the high Middle Ages and of the Renaissance.

Dr. Ong describes these agonistic structures as composed of four elements. The first was that of oral disputation. Students recited; they seldom wrote papers. They stood and defended their theses in loud clear voices or they attacked the school solutions. The professor was the sounding board, the sparring partner, and in the end the judge with authority who awarded the palm of praise or delivered the knockout blow. It was a dialectical process of argumentation through opposites, a ritual by which students learned subjects by fighting over them.

A second element was invariably a harsh physical regime. Classes started in darkness at 6 a.m., or before. The rules of behavior were strict. (Has anyone ever seen a schoolmaster portrayed in Renaissance art without his trusty bundle of switches at his side?) A third element of this agonistic structure was the pressure of constant translation; all of this oral disputation was conducted in the tribal language of intellectuals, Latin, the language of doctors and lawyers and metaphysicians. This language requirement in itself imposed a discipline, a structure, and a stressful learning situation. Ong says that the achievement of learning Latin, that tightly disciplined language, well enough to argue in it—indeed to defend one's academic reputation in it—became a sort of puberty rite for the Western-educated male in almost every century of this Christian era, save our own. The fourth element was the all-male character of this educational operation. Ong says that coeducation was incompatible with any of the elements above. I suppose that might be challenged by some educators today, but I am encouraged when I remember that today most advanced feminists will defend the viability of the single sex college, male or female. Ong's position seems reasonable to me when he argues that the agonistic style took shape in response to uniquely masculine needs.

The agonistic way, including test of manhood, has all but passed from the modern scene. But for what it's worth, as viewed by one who has presided over a single-sex institution where rites of passage are still observed, the self-imposed stress of a structured, disciplined, semi-autonomous student hierarchy yields many good results.

Education there becomes an irreversible process which equips its graduates with certain items of what some would call emotional baggage. Picked up along the way are concerns with loyalty, with commitment, a capacity for passion, for idealism. Such a stressful educational environment spurs a growth of conscience and also of salutary egoism.

Jacob Burckhardt, the 19th century Swiss historian, thought well of "that enigmatic mixture of conscience and egoism" he called honor. Although from many standpoints egoism is an impurity, and conscience alone would be nobler, he nevertheless acknowledged the utility and power of the blend. Egoism gives conscience staying power.

"Honor," writes Burckhardt, "is often what remains after faith, love, and hope are lost." (*The Civilization of the Renaissance in Italy,* London, 1929, p. 428.)

From my own experience, I think he's right. A sense of honor under pressure can outlast them all.

MORAL MAJORITY OR SERVANT MINORITY

by

Mark O. Hatfield

Senator Mark O. Hatfield

Senator Mark Hatfield has served in the U.S. Senate for thirteen years, after serving two terms as governor of Oregon, 1959–67. His governorship was marked by a program of "payrolls and playgrounds," as economic development of the state moved hand in hand with the state's environmental protection efforts. Hatfield also served Oregon as secretary of state, 1957–59, state senator, and state representative. After graduation from Willamette University in 1943 and Stanford University in 1948 with a bachelor's and a master's degree in political science, he taught political science at Willamette University and also served as dean of students, 1948–56. During World War II, he was a Lieutenant J.G., commanding landing craft at Iwo Jima and Okinawa.

Hatfield is the chairman of the Rules and Administration Committee.

Because he represents a state where the federal government owns over 50 percent of the land, Senator Hatfield's prime areas of expertise include natural resource and public land issues. His service on the Senate Appropriations Committee and the Senate Energy and Natural Resources Committee provides daily involvement in energy-related areas, forestry, housing, and water resource development.

As a leading Christian layman, Senator Hatfield has been a critic of "civil religion." He has written extensively for religious publications. Hatfield is the author of three books, Not Quite So Simple *(1967),* Conflict and Conscience *(1971), and* Between a Rock and a Hard Place *(1976), and coauthor of* Amnesty: The Unsettled Question of Vietnam *(1973).*

MORAL MAJORITY OR SERVANT MINORITY

by

Senator Mark O. Hatfield

I am grateful for the Cecil Lecture Series which provides me the opportunity to share a few observations on this election year. I am deeply honored to be here under such prestigious sponsorship. The dignity and the great personal charm of the Cecil family, their public dedication to this institution, to the legal profession, and to the people of this nation make it a high privilege, indeed, for a person in public office to speak under such good offices.

1980 was a very unique political year, not because of the results alone, but because we heard fundamentalist preachers claiming that the country was going to hell and that the only way Christians could respond to this situation was to elect Christians and legislate morality. These voices had been expressed through various organizations. Paul Wyrich, for the Committee for the Survival of a Free Congress, spoke openly about the commitment to "christianize" the government, to "christianize" America, and to get rid of people such as George Bush and others who did not agree with them on their moral basis. The Christian Voice became one of the registers of moral quotients applied to those in public office when it published a voting record that was to give an assessment based upon particular votes. I hate to confess that I flunked badly. I got only 23 percent on that schedule of issues. My colleague on the House side, Richard Kelly, who was indicted under the ABSCAM investigation, got

100 percent. Consequently, we have had that injection of a new religious awakening and awareness by what has come to be known as the Christian, evangelical, born-again, right-wing conservative group. This group has its certain hot-button issues that are immediate, emotional, and, of course, highly moral.

Some of my friends and colleagues on the liberal side of the religious spectrum, such as William Sloane Coffin of Riverside Church, a longtime friend and formerly a chaplain at Yale University, have become very concerned about the emergence of the religious right, wringing their hands with great predictions of evil to come. As a Republican liberal (understanding that labels are not very satisfactory), I don't believe that we can be concerned about participatory democracy and then be offended by those who have become interested and involved in the democratic process when they are not of our own political persuasion. So, let me say at the very onset that I welcome all who have come to feel and understand that they have Christian responsibilities and that they have citizenship responsibilities. Perhaps they merge in the point of involvement in our electoral process. "Come one, come all," is my view about people becoming involved in the political process.

But there are some unique characteristics about this particular group. First, unlike the liberal churchmen (who have been trying to influence political issues for many years, who have been involved in single-issue campaigns, and who have been raising moral application to political questions),, they have today 1,400 of the 8,000 American radio stations. Christian television takes in about one-half billion dollars a year from 50 million viewers. The top three television electronic preachers each gross nearly twice as much as the Republicans and the Democrats spent on the last presidential election. These are significant factors. The simple proposition that this group has a communications system makes it unlike most other pressure groups or other special interest groups.

I think it is also interesting to recognize that we can learn from history. And we should read more history. I read a very interesting essay written by a Canadian professor, Robert Allen Cook, who did a study on the ill-fated Weimar Republic following World War I in Germany. He drew some parallels to what he saw as certain forces emerging on the political scene in America over the last decade. In this study, there were certain essential characteristics noted that a democracy must address in order to keep it from degeneration. One of these was the resistance that we must always raise to atomization, which reduces a mass movement into frightened and isolated people who no longer identify with traditional values. Fearful souls flocked to the Nazi banner, and even industrialists and bankers contributed great sums of money to Hitler, because they saw in him a cohesive force in an otherwise impotent society. A breakdown in pluralism and individual values leads to mass movements with quick and ready simplistic solutions. It is interesting to note that when democracies decline, the mediating structures in a society, such as churches and unions and small businesses, local governments and political parties, which temper the individual's relationship to the rest of society, tend to erode and break down.

It is essential for us to recognize that there have been some radical changes occurring in the sagging role of our intermediate institutions in America since the 1930s.

For instance, today organized labor—American unions that represent labor—represent only one-fifth of the total labor force, whereas in the 1940s they represented one-third of the labor force of America. The role, the power, and the influence of the mediating force of the labor unions are diminishing. We find that it is increasingly difficult for the small entrepreneur, as well as the medium-sized entrepreneur, to stay in the mainstream of American economic life because they are being absorbed by the giant corporations. I grew up in a state where as a boy we referred to the majority of our timber operators as "gypo-loggers." That's a phrase of which my youngsters have no understanding, because the owner-operated gypo-logging firm has disappeared from the Oregon timber-oriented economy.

I have nothing *per se* against large corporations. But when the day comes that only the Georgia Pacifics, the Crown Zellerbachs, and the Weyerhaeusers can be operating in the state of Oregon to the exclusion of all other operators, it is a danger to all of us. We need the mix of small and medium-sized entrepreneurial enterprises. That is part of our mediating economic structure. We also see the growth and proliferation of large, authoritarian religious cults filling the vacuum as they appeal to the powerless. Even the electronic church is skimming off some of the resources that would go to the local small congregations. These facts hint serious implications.

Second, Cook undertook to demonstrate that a society to remain strong must be resistant to the apathy which was so characteristic of the Weimar Republic, where the far right (Nazis) emerged to challenge the far left (Communists), while the great middle group of people was crushed in between, mostly out of apathetic and apolitical attitudes. I feel today that the most set-upon class of people in America is the middle-income group, and this fact is leading to greater apathy. We find in the tax laws of this nation, in the overregulation of the federal government, and in many of these other factors an erosion of the middle-income group—the stability of any political society. And we find apathy toward political life. Barely over 50 percent of the people voted for the selection of a President of the United States. This very year, in the state of New York, in a very hotly contested primary election, only 37 percent of the eligible voters turned out to vote—little over one-third. So there are many evidences of an apathetic attitude amongst many people—disenchantment with institutions of government, disenchantment with institutions of education, disenchantment with the traditional family relationships.

Third, a strong democratic society must satisfy its people's hunger for wholeness with something other than the avant-garde culture and sexual license under which run dark currents of despair. Need I recite the fact that in pre-World War II Germany there was glorification of death and suicide undergirded with perfunctory mandatory prayer and religious instruction in the public schools, oftentimes linked with the Nazi ideology? Today in America suicide ranks as the third leading cause of death among teenagers. There are many other factors and data that we could use to illustrate that there is a longing and a void in the feeling of purpose and direction, not only in individual lives but in the corporate life of this nation.

This is the stage that brings us to the 1980 elections.

What do we mean when we hear that the answer to all of this—which President Carter referred to as a "malaise," which others referred to as a "sense of disconnectedness"—is the religious right's effort to fill this vacuum?

First, let me suggest that it might be helpful for you to know a bit about my background because I think we are all victims or products to a great degree of our experience and our environment. I come from the evangelical Christian community, having been reared in it as a Baptist. Saying you are a Baptist really doesn't say much, does it? There are so many kinds of Baptist. I am reminded of when Harry Truman, one of our Baptist Presidents along with Warren Harding, before Jimmy Carter, was asked at a press conference, "What kind of a Baptist are you, Mr. President?" Without hesitation he responded, "I'm a Bourbon Baptist." Well, that is not one of the classifications listed in Mead's *Handbook of American Denominations*. Someone else said what Baptists really are: "They are people who do not drink . . . in front of each other." I happen to come out of a Baptist background, but that really doesn't, as I said, tell you everything.

In World War II, as a young naval officer right out of Midshipmen's School, I happened to be assigned to that best of all admiral's assignments, an amphibious landing craft. I proceeded to report to Coronado Beach, California, where I was assigned as a wave commander. I had such naivete at tha time that I thought I was going to order some female sailors around—Waves, that is. But it was not really that kind of a command I was to take, but rather a wave of LCVPs that would hit the beaches at Iwo and Okinawa. And afterwards to fight in Indochina with Ho Chi Minh, our ally against Japan, and later to fight with Chiang Kaishek in Tientsin

Peking in the China civil war. I only mention that because oftentimes we are identified with short-hand descriptions; I am usually identified as one of the Senate "doves," whatever that means. But I also want it clearly understood that I believe in strong military preparedness and military defense. But I refuse to consider our national security as exclusively a military question. It's much broader than that, and much more complex. I think we should learn from the Shah of Iran what that mentality can lead us to—when our hardware becomes our sole hope or when every dollar addition we add to our military budget somehow increases our security by one dallar's worth. Again, those are myths that should be dispelled.

When we speak of the religious right, I feel that we have to realize that we are talking about a very sincere, dedicated group of Americans: ordinary people who have as much right to organize and to assert their political viewpoints as any other group in this nation. Bear in mind that the Constitution of the United States gives precisely the same rights to Madalyn Murray O'Hair that it gives to Billy Graham—no more, no less. And may it always be so. I say that because, again, I think we must maintain our constitutional commitment that this nation was founded on the basis of religious freedom. Among others, James Madison, as the great writer of religious freedom, had seen how the Baptists in his own colony of Virginia has been set upon, and he was aware of how the Massachusetts Bay Colony under the Puritans had driven out the Jews and the Quakers and the Baptists because they didn't conform. We have had our taste of religious intolerance. So I want to make sure that what I say has no bearing whatsoever on the political rights or any implication that I would circumscribe any of the political rights of any group in this nation which functions under the constitutional processes we have set up.

I think we have to realize that there are many single-issue groups today, not just the religious ones, and very frankly, I think it is due to the vacuum created by the two so-called major parties—Tweedledee and Tweedledum. Can you tell me why a Republican is a Republican by any standard philosophy or why a Democrat is a Democrat by any standard philosophy? As we read our political history, vacuums are what gave rise to third-party movements. An example is when the Democratic party failed to address the issue of slavery. And the Whig party failed to identify the issue of slavery. That gave birth to my political party, the Republican party, which was a conglomeration of Democrats, Free-Soilers, Whigs, Abolitionists, and others. Perhaps we are at the point today in America where the two-party system as you and I have known it is on the way out. Perhaps it is a time when, even though we Republicans feel this great, heady ecstasy over the results of the election, we may be in a transition that will move us to a multiparty system. The state of New York on this year's ballot had five political parties, fielding candidates from the state legislature to the United States Senate: the Democratic party, the Republican party, the Conservative party, the Liberal party, and the Right-to-Life party.

So the single issue, characteristic of the New Right, that has caused so much concern among many, is something that is far deeper than just a matter of religious issues. It has been in the making for quite some time.

I think we also have to realize that evangelical Christianity is a diverse group. It is not a monolithic group.

There are many evangelicals who share my concern that the grievous sins of our society are the corporate sins of militarism and materialism, rather than the so-called violation of the Taiwan Treaty or the support of ERA or of the Panama Canal Treaty. However, I must be very pointed in stating that I do have deep concern about those who attempt to baptize a religious dogma and create the impression that somehow God has given special revelation to a self-anointed group which then must promulgate that dogma and make it the criterion of another person's personal relationship to his God and to his faith. That is not in order as far as a pluralistic society is concerned. It divides not only the believer from the nonbeliever, but the believer from the believer as well. Again I come back to that fundamental point that the nonbeliever or the atheist or the agnostic has exactly the same rights under our political constitution as the believer. No group has the right to call into question one's personal relationship with God, one's religious commitment, on the basis or the criteria of political issues.

Certain activity is apostasy. It is apostasy because it substitutes a political gospel for a biblical gospel. If you want to understand the gospel as I believe the scripture clearly portrays it, the question is not what you think of the ERA, not what you think of the Panama Canal Treaty, not what you think of the Taiwan Treaty or sanctions on Rhodesian chrome. The Christian gospel consists of one question: What do you think of Jesus Christ? The gospel is a person. It is not a dogma, it is not a creed, it is not something we create for our own purposes to advance our own cause. Therefore, I think we have a responsibility within the Christian community to hold each other accountable for the false gospel we portray to the world that if you line up "correctly" on political issues you have bought yourself salvation or you have established your relationship to God. That is not biblical. It is heresy.

So I believe that this group, whether intended or not, is perceived as having made these issues the idols. The late president of Princeton Seminary, Dr. John McKay, once observed, "Whatever you make the issue, you make the idol."

It is very interesting, too, that even such an evangelical publication as *Christianity Today* (probably the great mouthpiece for the evangelical community) recently editorialized, raising flags of caution: "All evangelicals agree on very few things. One God, who in Christ chose to invade our planet in order to redeem men from sin. The substitutionary death of Jesus Christ on the cross, settling the score of man's sin; His own sovereign role of Supreme Judge of the universe; the need for a personal relationship with God through faith in Christ; and the call to discipleship and a life of sacrificial love. Everything else is application and secondary, even politics. Differences among Christians over fine points of theology or politics should be welcomed as a sign of breadth and vitality not of weakness." When I look at the efforts in the religious right to create a power base, it impresses me that perhaps the compelling motive is to defeat Caesar by becoming Caesar. And that's exactly what Jesus himself rejected. For remember that Satan's trump temptation was to deliver into Jesus's hands the kingdoms of the world and the glory that they would bring. But our Lord scorned the mastery founded on any sovereignty but servanthood: the servant leader. He even to this day bids us to take up the Cross and not the cudgel.

The response of Jesus defines forever that the Christian's relationship to the world is not control and power but ministry, the ministry of reconciliation, the ministry of healing, the ministry of bringing food and shelter to the helpless and to the poor outside of the mainstream. It's very interesting that if we look at both the Old Testament and New Testament scriptures, there is no one example given more frequently of God's criteria of judging our righteousness than that on the basis of our relationship to the poor. Read the Year of the Jubilee under the ancient Hebrews of the Old Testament and read the prophets Jeremiah and Isaiah and note their eloquence. The great prophet Isaiah said, "I note that you go into the temples and offer your oblations and your sacrifices and your prayers." But he said, "I see little evidence of your religion in the marketplace." He was standing there in the marketplace calling for the kind of application of compassion that was represented by the Year of the Jubilee; that was represented by leaving fallow ground every seventh year or by leaving a row of the olive trees or a part of the fields for the gleaners to be fed along with the poor. Thus our rich Jewish tradition and the heritage of our Judeao-Christian faith instruct us well about the imperatives of faithful witness in our society.

There is another factor that must be recognized by those who represent the Christian right, and that is the danger of the over-idealization of American history. They present George Washington kneeling at Valley Forge, Thomas Jefferson being like Moses the lawgiver, and Abraham Lincoln fulfilling the role of the Christian martyr. Many Christian conservatives have unwittingly exaggerated the role of religion in American history, making America God's nation of the New Covenant. There is an organization in this group called Citizens for God and Country. A preacher in Georgia made the headlines by claiming exclusivity for the Christian religion and that all other religions were against the law. Let me just say that many of our Founding Fathers were deists at best, children of the enlightenment, not children of the Reformation. In today's language they were the humanists of that day—which is a code word that the Christian right finds very obnoxious.

I think that there is always a role that God plays in the affairs of people. I do not deny the role that God plays in history. He is a God of history, he is a sovereign God. But to somehow create the impression that we have a special relationship that puts America above or outside the realm of accountability is not biblical. I think we must remember this, that our Founding Fathers were determined that we would have a religiously pluralistic nation. Without the recognition of the sound view that a person must be free in this nation not to believe, the idealization of history becomes spiritual justification for blind patriotism. Without this caution, America could be turned into a nation of religious bigots or one reminiscent of a medieval Christian state or a modern religious theocracy.

Also in this critique we must raise the element of arrogant intolerance. Perhaps, this is the most frightful dark side of the movement. There are some fond of quoting the scripture that "When the righteous rule, the people rejoice, and when the unrighteous rule, the people mourn." I would like to add, as one editorial writer added, "When the self-righteous rule, watch out." I think this intolerance of opposition or opponents is one which drives barriers between believers and nonbelievers. In a free society everything that is immoral does not have to be declared illegal. Through the years of our history we have come to expect religious rhetoric in an election year as unavoidable. But we do not have to settle for a religion of demagoguery, fear, bias, and imposition rather than the biblical religion of justice, mercy, compassion, and peacemaking. Especially if we compute biblical imperatives and injunctions, we find that most have to do with eliminating poverty and creating a more just society, focused on the poor, the oppressed, the imprisoned, the widows, and the orphans.

You might ask, if this environment exists today and the religious right is attempting to provide some kind of solution, what do you offer? What is the alternative to the religious right's approach?

First of all, Meg Greenfield of *Newsweek*, who I think has probably one of the most analytical, perceptive minds in the field of journalism today, wrote recently, "Government-grown values are by definition and necessity spiritually deformed. They tend to be lowest-common-denominator generalities or pressure-group-cooked outrages . . . But we have become so tolerant we have refused to view any indecency, outrage, or pathological assault on our sense of rightness in any way but a civil-liberties problem." I would have to agree, and would add that I do not believe that we can remove religion from society without grave consequences. But neither can we embrace an idolatry that reduces religion to merely the glue of society. Rather than a moral majority what is called for today is a redemptive minority, a minority which reflects on contemporary events in light of scriptural teaching and the tradition of boundless concern that justice be done to the needy.

Let me illustrate: We have about thirteen basic raw materials and minerals upon which our American superindustrial machine depends. What we see today in the energy field is but a tip of the iceberg. When we go through the U.S. Geological Survey and begin to analyze the sources of these minerals and raw materials, we find that beginning in about 1950 we were starting to import more of certain of these minerals than we had in the past. In fact, we were import-dependent for more than 50 percent of three of the thirteen. In 1960, that grew to five, and in 1980 it will climb to nine. By the year 2000, we will be importing at the present rate of consumption more than 50 percent, and in some instances nearly 90 to 100 percent, of twelve of the thirteen basic raw materials and minerals we need for our industrialized economy.

Now some of these needs may be met by new discoveries and explorations in Alaska if we are but wise in the way we legislate the future land use there. Even so, we still face the proposition that we live on a finite globe with finite resources. Let me suggest this, that we are a wasteful, exploitive, imperialistic nation as it relates to raw materials. We have assumed that we have an indispensable need and that we have an inexhaustible supply. We are cutting timber today at a greater rate than we are reforesting this nation. We had 200 million acres of land that once produced under private ownership timber that has been stripped from the land—now no timber growing whatsoever. Fifty-one percent of my state is owned by the federal government, the biggest timber-producing state of any of the fifty states. At the rate of cutting today, we will be denying the future generations even the basic raw material of timber.

The moral implication of this is that we are a wasteful people. We are not upholding the scriptural admonition of stewardship. We may translate that word into modern jargon and call it conservation. But let me assure you of this, that unless somehow we have a spiritual rebirth in this nation, even as it relates to raw materials and natural resources, and once again establish the biblical teaching of stewardship, we are going to be an impoverished nation and we are going to have greater vulnerability. All the bombs we can build, all the MX missiles we can create, and all the deadly weapons—neutron bombs—will not save us. General Dwight David Eisenhower, a five-star general, once observed, "There comes a time in a nation's life when an additional dollar spent for rockets and bombs and military hardware at a time when people are hungry and not fed, cold and not clothed, instead of increasing national security, will actually weaken national security." The vulnerability of America today is not in the lack of a military arsenal. The vulnerability of America is in the dependence upon imported oil. The vulnerability in national security of America is in economic inflation and low productivity. Until those are corrected, all the great escalation for more bombs is but developing another counterproductive Maginot Line mentality.

It was even a hard-liner like John Foster Dulles who said, "Unless there is a will and a strength in the people and a productivity in the economy, all the bombs we have will not save us."

What I am suggesting is not an either/or. It is simply a recognition of balance. It is a recognition of the moral implication in the issue. What we are trying to do today is find political and economic solutions to what are basically spiritual problems of stewardship. We have erected false gods in our economy. We have erected a false god of convenience and a false god of disposability. We want convenience and disposability in the marketplace, and every major technical decision we have made since World War II involving the product marketplace, the products we use, has been at energy-increased cost. Energy-cost effectiveness has not been considered. We have moved from the free-solar-energy-grown natural fibers of cotton and wool to the synthetic fibers, from soap to detergent, from the solar-replenished timber building materials that dominated the marketplace to light metals, glass, plastic, mortar, and all the things that have a heavy energy requirement.

So there is a moral implication. When others are scrounging to stay alive, have we a right to demand convenience and disposability, especially in those parts of the world on which we are growing more dependent for the raw materials, when we have exploited our own and now come to exploit theirs? Do you think they will continue to allow this rapacious lifestyle we have? Oh, I know that this sounds threatening to some people. I don't intend it to be threatening. I am not suggesting that we have to reduce our standard of living, our consumption standard from three square meals a day. Rather, I am talking about style of consumption. The costly and wasteful prepackaged, minimal-portion purchasing rather than bulk or cooperative buying is the habitual and convenience-oriented style of hurried Americans. We could feed the nation of Canada by the food we waste in garbage pails and disposals.

So it seems to me that a political position that does not recognize the moral implications and, therefore, ignores

the ultimate solutions is no wiser than one which tries to give simplistic religious solutions to complex economic and political problems. One of the perceptive writers of our day is Jeremy Rifkin. He speaks to this issue in a very interesting book *(Entropy)* that I would urge you to read. Rifkin, who is Jewish in his faith, says this: "If the Christian community fails to embrace the concept of a new-covenant vision of stewardship, it is possible that religious fervor could be taken over and ruthlessly exploited by right-wing and corporate interests. The evangelical awakening could end up providing the essential cultural backdrop that a fascist movement in the United States would require to maintain control during a period of long-range economic decline."

In concert with Rifkin's observations, it is my desire to issue a call to a thoroughgoing and modern biblical faith that puts aside a theology of rapacious consumerism to embrace a theology of the sacredness of life, conservation, protection, and sharing of God's creation.

So perhaps we should say thank you to the so-called New Right for having raised some of these political, moral, and religious issues that tend to alarm or confuse or concern people. Let us take this then as a positive step to assess our own position and our own philosophy, to see wherein we may learn. And perhaps do better. I believe there are moral implications in most political and economic issues. I would be hesitant, though, to try to put forth a list, because then it would be the same kind of arrogance that I criticize in others who set forth their lists and expect everyone else to comply.

May I just close with these thoughts: The Lord has called us to salvation not safety, to make a covenant with life not death, and in the struggles and ambiguities of this calling he promised to provide for us a refuge that refreshes and gives courage for the challenges to come.

I take great hope, I have great faith that we can come through this challenging time. I belive that perhaps this election, more than any since 1932, signals a new direction. Now we have to have not only the men and the women of faith and hope, trust and confidence, to give leadership, but those within the citizen body to give support and "followership," so that truly we not only address the great issues of this day but also understand the deep implications that we have been given a moment of history that will be a hinge event on which the door will swing one way or the other. If we are but wise, knowledgeable, compassionate, and reconciling in nature, we can give this kind of role to each person.

MORAL VALUES IN BUSINESS-GOVERNMENT RELATIONS

by

Joe H. Foy

Joe H. Foy, Esq.

Born in the South and having served the citizens of San Angelo, Houston, and Texas as city attorney and school board president, president of the Houston Grand Opera Association, and vice-chairman of the Texas Turnpike Authority (respectively), Mr. Foy is a Partner of the Houston law firm, Bracewell and Patterson.

Mr. Foy was associated with the Houston Natural Gas Corporation for fifteen years, and served as president, chief operating officer, and vice-chairman of that corporation. The Vanderbilt Law School alumnus is well known for his expertise in matters relating to energy, natural resources, and the ramifications of government regulation.

A member of the Board of Directors of Cooper Industries; Texas Commerce Bank, Lakeside; Lifemark Corporation; Gulf Coast Savings Association; and the Central and South West Corporation, Mr. Foy also serves on the board of St. Thomas University, the executive committee of the Houston Chamber of Commerce, and is the public councilor of the Texas A&M Research Foundation.

Mr. Foy is a Charter Fellow of the Texas Bar Foundation and has authored various legal articles relating to utilities and federal regulations.

MORAL VALUES IN BUSINESS-GOVERNMENT RELATIONS

by

Joe H. Foy

A strong case can be made for the proposition that American business is heavily overregulated by government. This can be interpreted—and has been by some—as the work of an insidious conspiracy inspired by the motive to destroy the free enterprise system. There is indeed a philosophy which regards business as essentially amoral, if not immoral, in its natural tendencies, and holds that strict governmental supervision of the details of its operations is essential to protect the public welfare. Opinion polls taken among the American public are extremely unflattering to the businessman; however, the standing in public opinion of government officials is hardly any better. Naturally, those who deal at first hand with the bureaucracies are prompt to point out much that is foolishly burdensome in the web of regulatory measures which they have spun.

There can be no doubt that most American business enterprises operate within a maze of governmental restrictions and requirements. One major natural gas corporation with 24 domestic subsidiaries recently identified no less than 100 federal, regional, and state agencies with which it must deal on a regular basis. A study prepared for the Joint Economic Committee of the United States Congress reported that in 1976 the American business sector spent $62.9 billion in order to comply with federal regulations alone. That amounts to $300 for each man, woman, and child in the United States.

That same study asserted that "the cost of operating federal regulatory agencies is rising more rapidly than the budget as a whole, the population, or the gross national product." There are over 4,400 different federal forms which the private sector must fill out each year, requiring over 143 million man-hours of work. The deflection of $10 billion of capital spending to meet federal environmental, safety, and similar regulations deprives the economy of investments that could increase the annual level of growth in productivity by one-third, according to one economist quoted in the study. This is occurring in an era when the most serious need in combatting an apparently endemic inflation is to increase the productivity of American enterprise.

These are facts that warrant our attention. However, they do not really explain how and why such a situation has developed, whether it is the result of an invidious immorality among businessmen, or whether it is a foolish invasion of free enterprise prerogatives. They do show that the country has come a great distance away from the philosophy of Jefferson that that government is best which governs least, and the laissez-faire economic theories of Adam Smith, who wrote his famous *Wealth of Nations* in the same year that Jefferson wrote the American Declaration of Independence.

There is, of course, a morality which exists in the absence of law. In his theological masterpiece, the "Epistle to the Romans," Paul, the apostle, observed that there were those who, not having been under law, became "a law unto themselves." They observed natural ethical standards, to which they conformed in the utter absence of compulsion. On the other hand, he found the law (of Moses) impossible for mankind literally to comply with. Had there been no law, he would not have known sin. It is better and easier to do right because it is right than to do right because it is commanded. Human nature needs to be free of artificial constraints, for only then can it express its true moral character.

Outside of the theological realm, however, is it truly possible for business to become "a law unto itself"? Admittedly, in an ideal world of ideal humans, regulation would not have to exist at all—in fact, there would be no need for any kind of law.

Adam Smith supported the laissez-faire doctrine for another reason. The self-interest of individual businessmen, he taught, would lead them, if free, to conduct their businesses in the overall best interest of the public. Carried to its logical conclusion, this would mean that a businessman would not deal in shoddy merchandise, because his trade would suffer as a result—that he would not work his labor force at inferior wages or under harmful or dangerous conditions, because that would impede their efficiency—that he would not pollute the environment, because he had to live in it as a member of the same public that he has a self-interest in protecting. Unfortunately, neither natural morality nor wholesome self-interest has demonstrated these salutary results in practice.

One of the elements of self-interest is greed, "that disease of which all old men sicken—avarice." (Middleton, *The Roaring Girl,* Act 1, Sc. 1.) Shakespeare's "itching palm" is common to all but saints, of whom there are few. The decades of the Industrial Revolution following the publication of Adam Smith's classic did not at all demonstrate that the coincident self-interest of businessmen would promote the welfare of the whole. It would be more accurate to say that the laissez-faire system survived in spite of itself and principally because political power was denied to the masses of consumers and laborers who provided its production and its markets.

Thus, governmental regulation of business arose and grew because, in some respects, business failed to provide goods and services satisfactorily and at reasonable prices to the public and because, in other respects, business failed adequately to communicate its best results to the public and its representatives, and also because economic forces moved in uncontrollable and unpredictable ways to the detriment of individual businesses and their investors. Most regulation has little or nothing to do with traditional moral principles, and its existence reflects no kind of judgment upon the philosophical morality of the regulated business. The situation as it exists today is probably an inescapable result of the contemporaneous development of representative government and a massive, privately owned enterprise system in this country over the past 200 years.

Frederick Jackson Turner, the historian of the American frontier, found in that historical phenomenon the influences that gave their shape to modern American social and political institutions. With no colonial foundation to build upon, the frontier states experimented with innovative state and local governmental structures and procedures. The abundant cheap land attracted imaginative and venturesome people, who faced in common a rigorous and dangerous environment. An egalitarian attitude brought about universal suffrage, as well as many other measures designed to foster independence and parity among individuals. A variety of economic differences bred among these people deep distrust and scorn for the Eastern banking and industrial establishments.

In time, the abundant land was fully appropriated, but the conditions and attitudes it had spawned still lived. Eventually, the Populism of the West and South found common expression with developing forces of Eastern liberalism in the reform legislation of the thirties and forties.

While the frontier developed, open immigration policies brought entire new classes from Ireland, Italy, Germany, Poland, and elsewhere into the metropolitan areas of the Northeast and the Midwest. Habituated to hard work, they were an important source of labor; they tended to gather in ethnic neighborhoods; they were generally poor; and they were subject to organization for political objectives.

By the thirties, popular election of United States Senators had developed a brigade of independent and powerful voices in the legislative forum, the forces of labor were beginning to flex electoral muscle, and a vast popular combination confronted the industrial domination of earlier eras with superior voting power.

It would have been surprising if these historical developments had not led, in the depression years, to sweeping economic changes through legislation. Investor and Presidential Advisor Bernard M. Baruch would later identify the four most important economic measures as (1) social security, (2) unemployment insurance, (3) federal deposit insurance, and (4) securities and securities exchange regulation. Many other specific kinds of regulatory legislation arose from the New Deal. More important than any particular set of statutes, however, was the adoption by a majority of the electorate of an idea that had long been brewing: that government has a responsibility for the welfare of its citizens beyond providing for the common defense, building roads, bridges, and harbors, and printing currency.

Laissez-faire economics had indulged in its last fling during the Harding, Coolidge, and Hoover Administrations. The basic governmental structure of the country would never be the same. Self-interest would never again be completely trusted to promote the public interest. Indeed, Franklin Roosevelt said in his second inaugural address: "We have always known that heedless self-interest was bad morals; we know now that it is bad economics."

American business would have to adjust to a completely new set of ground rules, applicable to its structure, its capitalization, its labor policies, and its products and services. Without attempting extensive analysis, this paper asserts that, notwithstanding the many difficulties and frustrations caused by the regulatory trend, on the whole, the American economic system is stronger, fairer, and better, American business is more prosperous and secure, and the individual consumer and laborer better protected than if those sweeping changes had not taken place.

Such a conclusion does not imply any broad condemnation of the moral standards of business or businessmen. It simply recognizes that the regulatory pressure has forced improvements in the economic system which have made it a more effective and a fairer system. To demonstrate the truth of the proposition, one merely needs to remember the times of the system as it was in a simpler past:

A time without federal deposit insurance and without regular federal or state examinations of the banks to which we entrust our money in deposits.

A time when promoters could sell securities with nothing but the blue sky behind them, without even the obligation to make full and fair disclosure of assets, liabilities, earnings, and material business developments, in which insiders could profit at the expense of the public on information not generally known.

A time when children and women worked 18-hour days for pennies and when the workingman had little power over the conditions, hours, or wages of his labor.

A time when the land, the air, and the water were despoiled in the exploitation of natural resources and the disposal of industrial wastes.

A time when poisonous food and drugs were dispensed with no safeguards to an unsuspecting public.

A time without social security benefits for the aged and without public support for the involuntarily unemployed.

Out of the matrix of the thirties came an intensive examination of the American economic system, involving the universities and the university-trained economist, financial expert and management specialist to a tremendous new extent. There have followed 50 years in which quantitative studies of the system have multiplied to levels never before imagined. Economic experts have become institutionalized in business, government, and the media.

From a minor role in the university curriculum, the American graduate school of business has grown to become a prolific degree factory. Although there were few such institutions 50 years ago, today hardly any respectable American university is without such a school. Today's business executive is far better informed than his predecessors about the country's financial and economic institutions and the legal and social climate in which he must operate, as well as about the management and operating techniques that have proven most successful.

The explosion of information and training in these decades paralleled the astounding growth of scientific and technological knowledge. It could be boasted in 1976 that more scientists and engineers were then alive than had lived in all the history of the world before the twentieth century. Thousands of university graduates have elected to concentrate in the relatively new fields of public health and hygiene and environmental safety.

Today's tractor retailer is expected to provide a better understanding of his machines, their parts and accessories, than the manufacturer of the product in his grandfather's era. A host of products which would have been dismissed as mere imaginative chimeras 50 years ago are important components of the marketplace.

There is no excuse in 1980 for an investor to make the kind of uninformed judgment that his grandfather might have made when he risked his nest egg in one of Samuel Insull's utility holding companies. Bank directors are constantly apprised through examiners' reports of the bank's capital position, the safety of its operating procedures, and the quality of its loan portfolio. Every management of every publicly held company is forced by the discipline of financial reporting to both public agencies and private financial analysts to have a better understanding of its own financial and operating policies and their results.

The proliferation of knowledge itself is a powerful influence upon the moral standards that a modern business executive must observe. Not only what business knows, but also what it is expected to know, is taken into account when business actions are judged.

Adam Smith could explain the division of labor by the homely illustration of a pin factory. As basic teaching, his illustration remains valid. It hardly touches upon the complex decisions which must be made by the manager of a chemical plant whose raw materials are carcinogenic or whose wastes are poisonous, or of a nuclear plant which needs inherently redundant equipment and procedures to avoid possible wholesale loss of life or danger to health.

Knowledge has therefore produced a higher ethical standard for business than ever existed before even the decade of the 1970s. The old moral battles against the effects of unrestrained greed or of fraud or exploitation are still with us. However, the businessman can no longer rely on simple obedience to the commandments:

> Thou shalt not cheat.
>
> Thou shalt not misrepresent the quality of the product.
>
> Thou shalt not operate a sweat shop or abuse children or women in your labor force.

There is a more profound and a subtler obligation.

One of the unfortunate side effects of regulation is that it tends to disguise this subtler obligation. Having been confronted with a regulation and having complied with it to the letter, one has a tendency to assume that all his ethical obligations have been met. Regulation instills a false sense of comfort and a welcome apparent opportunity to shift the reponsibility of planning to a public agency. In this sense, regulation can be corruptive. It can destroy the initiative to develop the public interest, just as it often is necessary to protect it.

Regulated industries can become so comfortable with a regulatory system that they would no more let it go than would a child his rubber duck or his little blanket. Some executives in the airline industry were startled to find that the new freedom of unregulated competition could compensate their enterprises handsomely for the supposed loss of security; others have had difficulty in adjusting. Trucking executives may learn the same lesson, now that deregulation of trucking has become a reality. Undoubtedly, the stagnation of many American railroads occurred because managements developed a mentality which regarded conformity as the whole of duty.

Intense regulation begets another error, which is the elevation of appearances over realities. Corporate lawyers become well-disciplined in the art of seeing that the records of proceedings and transactions reflect exact compliance with rules that were not so strictly observed in substantive discussions. Thus, attention is distracted by adherence to forms rather than to the substantive long-range benefit of both a business and its public.

Thus, regulation and regulatory procedures tend to take on a life of their own, independent of the evils they were designed to inhibit, and often outliving them. In the modern era, there is virtually no chance that the evils of early public utility holding company systems could occur again, whether or not the Public Utility Holding Company Act of 1935 were still on the books, yet the strictures of the Act continue to bind the planning and the operations of its subject companies in a generation when energy companies most need to direct their efforts toward economies and sufficiency of production. Perhaps the worst feature of regulatory legislation is its propensity for eternal life, surviving forever after the demise of the vices which gave it its genesis.

While the businessman is apparently quite capable of adjusting to a heavily regulated existence—indeed thriving within its sway—his customers may find that the higher costs reflected in prices and the disinclination toward innovative planning and product development are dismal results of a system intended for their benefit. It is doubtful that the years of natural gas wellhead price regulation in interstate commerce after the first *Phillips* decision of 1954 or the controls on domestic oil and products prices imposed by the Nixon Administration in 1973 have accomplished any lasting public good whatever. They probably intensified shortages and dislocated markets in such a way as to result in higher prices than would exist today had they never been imposed.

There should be—and there someday may be—a morality in business based not on regulation but on knowledge, diligence, and the careful consideration of mutual benefit for the enterprise and the public. Such a Utopian state would arise from the continuing development of knowledge and the growth of a spirit of cooperation, rather than confrontation between business and the public. It would be the product of voluntary dedication of management to the longer range benefit of the company, based upon a continuing improvement in the company's service to the public and a pervasive respect for the public welfare.

Of course, the knowledge required to meet such a standard cannot be stored in one or a few brains. It would be necessary for the entire business organization to attain such competency in all the disciplines involved and to cooperate so smoothly as to bring the best and most recent information to bear upon every major business decision. What the standard really would require is a deeper moral commitment by management to the application of knowledge than has ever been made in the past.

To the extent that internal expertise were available, it would be called upon for its maximum contribution. Where needed, expert consultants would be employed. There is a place for consultation with regulatory staffs, who might bring a broad-gauged and disinterested viewpoint into the process.

This kind of moral standard is an ideal which is probably impossible of attainment, certainly extremely difficult. It is fascinating, however, to indulge in fantasy about one or two current national problems which might have been avoided by its application.

An eventual shortage of domestic crude oil was predictable (and indeed was predicted by the Paley Commission) by the early 1950s. Suppose that all American automobile manufacturers had taken that into account in their planning and had made fuel economy an important objective in automobile design. Perhaps they would have avoided a 25-year commitment in Detroit to ever heavier, larger cars. The finest advertising brains would have concentrated on selling cars on their maneuverability, ease of parking, and convenient handling, rather than their length, roominess, and speed.

By 1980, automobile fuel requirements would have been less than half the present level, and oil imports would be from 25 to 30 percent less than are currently required. The American public would not have had to turn to small automobiles imported from Germany and Japan. The balance of trade and the balance of payments might even be favorable to the United States, and the dollar much stronger against the most solid of foreign currencies.

For the automobile companies themselves, there would have been a steadier growth in sales and profitability. Chrysler would not be in such a precarious position, and perhaps American Motors' early commitment to smaller cars would have proven more successful in competition against the Big Three. Those workers recently laid off might have been steadily employed. Everyone, and, possibly most of all, the investors in automobile industry common stocks would have benefited.

It is no excuse to say that the country as a whole failed to foresee the need for fuel-efficient cars. Nothing is plainer than that oil is a depletable natural resource. While conservation seems contrary to an overconfident nation's basic beliefs, leadership has a duty to be more prescient than the average citizen. Unless business leadership accepts and performs that duty, it will inevitably find its decisions unfavorably reviewed in hindsight by the public and that government which represents the public.

Perhaps that illustration overtaxes frail human capability. However, would such decisions as the production of automobiles known to be explosive on rear-end collision or of radial tires known to fail, in the effort to prevent write-offs of expensive machinery, be viewed now as beyond mortal capacity to avoid? Would the managements involved again subject their companies to the risk of hundreds of millions of dollars in losses for the sake of the much smaller savings they temporarily achieved?

There is a moral value in prudence, in the employment of the best available knowledge to make sound long-range judgments. Business leaders have an obligation to look beyond the most convenient and immediate means of securing profits to the establishment of policies that will keep their enterprises in profitable service over a long future.

Unfortunately, the capacity for being short-sighted is not limited to the businessman's own company. In common with other interest groups, business executives have a seriously imperfect record in the area of public policy. Again, narrow, temporary self-interest tends to distort their vision.

Electric utility executives protested eloquently against the establishment in New Deal days of the Tennessee Valley Authority and the Rural Electrification Administraton. One of the most strident protestors was popular enough to be nominated for President in 1940. In retrospect, the TVA seems to have been a major cause for the growth of prosperity in the Southeast, and the REA a major contributor to the astounding productivity of American agribusiness, the crown jewel of our economy.

In order to obtain deregulation of new natural gas, the oil and gas industry was not loath to allow incremental pricing to be imposed on industrial gas customers. As the American Gas Association predicted, the incremental pricing provisions of the Natural Gas Policy Act are now generally viewed with dismay in industrial circles.

Blue Cross/Blue Shield insurance was bitterly resisted in the beginning by the American Medical Association. Later the AMA fought Medicare and Medicaid. No other factors have contributed more to the prosperity of the medical profession or to the security of the public in the face of soaring medical costs. Will the legal profession's long battle against dignified advertising prove to have been similarly inimical to its longer range interest? Professionals, no less than business executives, are capable of developing myopia.

Admittedly, the concepts developing in this paper go far beyond traditional ideas of morality. However, many aspects of morality are not necessarily relevant to the more important public effects of business activity. A lecher or an alcoholic may be able in spite of those faults to make sound decisions, produce useful products, and maintain a happy and secure labor force. Businessmen may lie to each other in major transactions between themselves without any effect whatever on the public; private legal remedies are available to redress private wrongs. "It is naught, it is naught, saith the buyer: but when he is gone his way he boasteth" (Proverbs 20:14).

On the other hand, the most pious, straitlaced, psalm-singing, almsgiving, churchgoing pillar of rectitude may be a pompous and ignorant fraud whose factory pollutes a stream or whose widgets are likely to explode and cripple their unsuspecting buyers. He may be, as Mark Twain put it, "a good man, in the worst sense of that word." The great authors, from Shakespeare to Sinclair Lewis and beyond, have taught us that a "good" man may be immoral in a public sense, a "bad" man highly moral. Lincoln's famous dictum about Grant's drinking habits readily comes to mind: he could wish all his generals would learn to drink Grant's brand.

Sermons are for Sunday. Business is generally conducted on other days of the week. Morality in business consists in public concern. For business, the public comprises its investors, its employees, its customers, and all those who may be affected by its activities. The moral businessman shows his concern for all of them by diligently planning for their mutual best interest.

By no means should the businessman ever overlook the objective of profitability. To do so betrays not only his investors but also those employees who depend on the success of the enterprise for jobs, as well as those consumers who depend upon the life of the enterprise for replacement parts and service.

It can almost be said that in the large enterprise there is a moral imperative not to fail. Many modern business enterprises are so large and so widespread, and have so many suppliers, employees, and customers—not to mention investors—that their collapse injures millions, and the rubble requires endless effort to clean up. This may seem a dreadful burden for the chief executive to bear, but he is well paid for it. Hardly any chief executive of a major U.S. corporation holds that office more than a few years without becoming wealthy.

As business enterprises grow ever larger, the public pressure to make them more efficient and more conscious of their responsibilities will intensify. Congressional investigators will hale more businessmen before their committees. Laws will continue to proliferate, and many of them will prove to be unsound.

Proposals to alter the basic systems of corporate governance will continue to thrive and multiply. Reformers are no longer content to regulate externally. The chairman of the Securities and Exchange Commission now advocates that only the chief executive officer should sit on the corporate board as an insider; all other members should be independent. Others advocate that representatives of labor, of consumers, and of the general public should sit on the board.

There has been a growing trend toward a majority of outside directors. The audit committee of the board—comprising only outsiders—has acquired immense new importance in a very short period. The Foreign Corrupt Practice Act has imposed significant new duties upon management, the board, and the audit committee in the development and diligent use of rigorous internal control procedures. Perhaps the corporation has made more progress in reforming its basic governance than in most other areas of responsibility.

It is doubtful whether depriving the board of knowledgeable insiders, on the theory that they will always be subservient to the chief executive officer, is beneficial where the board has a strong majority of outsiders. However, the danger of too much dominance by a strong-willed chairman is real, and boards need to guard against it. Proposals to stack the board with representatives of interests other than the shareholders would tend, it seems, toward a group schizophrenia. Special interest advocates would find themselves too often in conflicts of interest to be of much use as directors. There is good reason for the board to continue to examine itself, maintaining a proper control over business policy; there is no reason to impose rigid new systems of representation, which are likely to subvert the ability of the board to govern.

In every area of its concern, the modern business will escape regulation by government only to the extent it proves its ability to regulate itself. If the manager ignores evidence that working conditions are harmful to his workers' health, he can expect not only to respond in damages but to find regulatory supervisors in his plant as well. If he speculates too aggressively in a commodities market, disrupting normal economic patterns, he can expect to bring tighter trading controls on himself and everyone else as well. If he endangers his company's financial health, he is courting a receivership and a complete loss of his control.

There are intelligent and sound ways of responding to unwise proposals for laws and regulations. Inflexibility and intemperate criticism of Congress and the agencies are not among those ways. Congressman Eckhardt (D., Tex.) has identified three kinds of lobbyists. There is the "beef and bourbon" operator, who influences legislators by doing them favors and entertaining them. There is the "muscle" representative, who threatens the legislator with reprisals by an interest group if he does not do its will. Finally, there is the constructive analyst and supplier of information, who works patiently with the legislator and his staff, pointing out the deficiencies of a proposed statute and the factual considerations that require its amendment or defeat. The third is obviously not only the most helpful, but also the most effective, in the long run.

It has been a long time since Will Rogers opined that the only distinctive American criminal class was Congress. His accusation was as false as it was funny. Members of Congress, on the whole, probably work harder, are more patriotic and more honest than the average American.

Businessmen, as a class, do not deserve the pejorative description of them attributed to his father by President John F. Kennedy. More businessmen achieve more success through honorable than through dishonorable means. Both classes, businessmen and politicians, are widely condemned for the sins of relatively few of them. Each has a propensity for shrill invectives against the other, and that may be the worst failing of each.

Both business and government need to learn to cope with the system as it is and as it can be reasonably modified, not as they might wish it could have been. A few realists in the oil industry recognize that the so-called windfall profit tax is the price of a ticket to the phenomenal profits of decontrolled oil; many seem to believe the fashionable rhetoric of their association leaders. A few realists in Congress understand how recent deregulation and decontrol measures have stimulated domestic oil and gas exploration; many seem only to understand the higher cost they imposed on the consumer.

If businessmen can learn to spend their effort in conceiving, planning, and communicating constructive policies to the public, to Congress, and to the Administration rather than in denouncing the system and its components, they may accomplish far more in their defense against false accusations and bad regulations than they ever dreamed.

Thus, they could urge upon their representatives a more thorough consideration of the economic consequences of regulation, insisting that the cost of new requirements to the economy be weighed against their benefits.

They could urge that statutes and regulations be clearly stated and uniformly applied. It is often more important to know what the rules are, than to have a perfect set of rules to observe.

They could work most assiduously to bring an end to the inordinate delays in regulatory decisions—delays which impede constructive investment and enormously increase cost. They could insist that government be as efficient and candid as government insists that business must be.

They could pay more attention to laws and regulations in their formative stages, so that errors of innocent ignorance may be reduced.

They could open avenues of communication to public interest groups, to develop an appreciation of mutual objectives and an agreement on measures to accomplish common good.

They could participate actively, as individuals, in the elective process, to put in office candidates who are open to persuasion on public issues and to defeat demagogues and ideologues whose philosophy is to destroy rather than to build.

Most important, they could and must shape their own business policies in ways that demonstrably serve the interests of their customers, their shareholders, and the general public.

The perception of better moral values in American business would go far to alleviate many of its problems. It is not enough simply to run a business honorably with due regard for the public interest. Public concerns must also be communicated to the public. Institutional advertising and published addresses need to go beyond denunciation of governmental restrictions and praise of the free enterprise system. They must demonstrate what business itself is doing to improve its products, protect its workers and consumers, and contribute to constructive modifications of the system.

Moral values would hold their greatest significance in business-government relations when each side, business and government, would concentrate most intently on improving its own moral values. Government would not meddle needlessly with free enterprise; business would not waste its breath in shrill invectives against bureaucrats. "Eddie" might not be so mad. That is an ideal state which will never be reached, but it is worth reaching for.

EDUCATION FOR CITIZENSHIP

by

Andrew R. Cecil

Dr. Andrew R. Cecil

Dr. Cecil is Chancellor and Trustee of The Southwestern Legal Foundation and Distinguished Scholar in Residence at The University of Texas at Dallas, Texas.

Associated with the Foundation since 1958, Dr. Cecil has helped guide its development of five educational centers that offer nationally and internationally recognized programs in advanced continuing education.

In February 1979 the University established in his honor the Andrew R. Cecil Lectures on Moral Values in a Free Society, and invited Dr. Cecil to deliver the first series of lectures in November 1979. The first annual proceedings were published as Dr. Cecil's book The Third Way: Enlightened Capitalism and the Search for a New Social Order, *which received an enthusiastic response.*

Educated in Europe and well launched on a career as a professor and practitioner in the fields of law and economics, Dr. Cecil resumed his academic career after World War II in Lima, Peru, at the University of San Marcos. After 1949, he was associated with the Methodist church-affiliated colleges and universities in the United States until he joined the Foundation. He is author of twelve books on the subjects of law and economics and of more than seventy articles on these subjects and on the philosophy of religion published in periodicals and anthologies.

A member of the American Society of International Law, of the American Branch of the International Law Association and of the American Judicature Society, Dr. Cecil has served on numerous commissions for the Methodist Church, and is a member of the Board of Trustees of the National Methodist Foundation for Christian Higher Education. Dr. Cecil also serves as a member of the Development Board of The University of Texas at Dallas.

EDUCATION FOR CITIZENSHIP

by

Andrew R. Cecil

Two Kinds of Leadership

In the last two decades, educational institutions have not lived up to expectations in providing young people with the education for citizenship that will prepare them adequately to function in a democratic society beset by national and international problems unprecedented in their complexity. In the sixties, we were faced with growing student disorders that brought about crises on most of the campuses throughout the nation. Some tried to find comfort in the fact that campus unrest is not a new problem, since Plato had written that in a democracy "the schoolmaster fears and flatters the pupils." Others believed that the days of the traditional campus were numbered.

In the seventies, voices of skepticism accused institutions of learning of being knowledge factories turning out skilled professionals without regard to the traditional aims of liberal education. Our society has the right to expect that educational institutions will discharge their responsibility to prepare good, well-informed citizens, effectively participating in democracy, by exposing students to the moral questions arising in human relations. Such exposure is constructive since only well-informed, educated citizens have the ability to cope with the existing differences between theory and reality when they are faced with such problems confronting our society as the preservation of freedom and justice, the elimination of racial discrimination and poverty, and the search for stability and public order.

Since educational institutions have failed to discharge their responsibility, we have witnessed a taxpayers' rebellion which included resistance to added school taxes and new school bond issues. This taxpayers' "revolt" could be paralleled to the resistance of private sources of money whose support was solicited by the private segment of the academic world. The existence of private institutions is being challenged, and a transition from private to public control has occurred in a number of colleges and universities because of financial difficulties. (Between 1968 and 1978, eighty-seven private four-year colleges closed their doors.)

The continued support of taxpayers for public institutions and of private sources for private institutions may depend upon the public's being convinced that our schools, colleges, and universities have not abdicated their responsibility to shape the ideals and habits of our society. As Spinoza expressed it, "Men are not born for citizenship, but must be made fit for it." Because of the relevance of education to the building of a society able to recognize its problems, able to conceive for them effective solutions, and able to put those solutions into effect, we justly may expect that our educational institutions train future leaders responsible to the hopes and aspirations of the mass of people, who in a democracy ultimately shape the nation's destiny. When we refer to future leaders, let us point out two kinds of leadership.

As we look back through the pages of history, we can see that the destiny of the world has been shaped largely by men whose leadership was born in the heat of crisis. From the time of Moses, whose leadership was born in the face of the persecution of the Jews by the Pharaohs, to the present time, leadership has been born in the pain of slavery and exploitation, as a reaction against poverty and misery.

Let us take the history of this hemisphere. The leadership of George Washington would not have been the same had he not faced the crisis of the American Revolution. At age 19, Abraham Lincoln witnessed for the first time the sale of slaves at auctions, and the sight so moved him that he committed himself to abolish the slavery system. Before his resolution could be turned into the action of the Emancipation Proclamation, the entire United States had to suffer the crisis of civil war.

Simon Bolivar would not have become the leader he was in South America had he not been faced by the crisis of the exploitation of his compatriots by the Spanish conquerer. In the eyes of many Americans, Woodrow Wilson would not have achieved such great heights of leadership had he not been faced by the crisis of the First World War; nor would Franklin D. Roosevelt have held the great admiration of so many Americans had it not been for the great depression; nor would Dwight Eisenhower have had the same popularity had he not faced the Second World War, which gave him the glory of a victorious general.

We have mentioned some of the world leaders who directed their abilities toward the betterment and the welfare of their societies and the world. If by a leader we mean one who is followed by others in conduct and opinion, we can safely say that some types of leadership which in the course of history have proved to be disastrous were also born in the white heat of crises. Essentially, the conditions that produced the leadership of the "fuehrer" Adolf Hitler, the Duce Mussolini, and the "wozdz" (father of all nations) Joseph Stalin were the same: the economic and political disunity of the people and the hopelessness of the lower classes, who were willing to embrace any idea in an effort to better their conditions.

But there is a second kind of leadership which is greater than that which we have been discussing—greater and different from the leadership of kings and warriors, politicians and dictators—leadership to prevent crisis. There is the leadership of millions who have gone to their graves unknown although they changed the history of the world. We have in mind the leadership of millions who, in their daily life, through their conduct, and through their relations to their fellowmen, have prevented economic or political catastrophe. To provide this type of leadership which prevents crisis is the primary concern of education for citizenship.

This type of leadership is not founded on birth, wealth, or party membership. As Jefferson pointed out, "There is a natural aristocracy among men. The grounds of this are virtue and talents." This natural aristocracy, which Jefferson believed to be "the most precious gift of nature," calls not for egalitarianism but for vesting the responsibility for our destiny in the hands of educated men and women who excel in intellectual capacity and dedication to their fellowmen.

H. G. Wells, the English sociologist and historian, in his monumental work, *The Outline of History,* pointed out that human history becomes more and more a race between education and catastrophe. What is the role of education in this race to meet the challenge of the dynamically changing world? What is the role of education in the search for leadership to prevent crisis or catastrophe? Whether the miraculous inventions that play such an important part in our society shall be consecrated to man's life or dedicated to his death depends upon the goals we establish for our educational efforts. In establishing these goals it is well to remember the warning Moses gave to the Hebrews: "Behold, I set before you this day a blessing and a curse: the blessing, if you obey the commandments of the Lord your God, which I command you this day, and the curse, if you do not obey the commandments of the Lord your God, but turn aside from the way which I command you this day, to go after other gods which you have not known" (Deuteronomy 11: 26-28).

Benjamin Disraeli in his speech before the House of Commons, June 15, 1874, declared: "Upon the education of the people of this country the fate of this country depends." Since ancient times, the purpose of education has been to make the minds of children fitted to cope with the problems of their environment. Socrates taught that a rightly trained mind would naturally turn toward virtue. The "right training" calls not only for intellectual development but also for spiritual perception in order to understand God's creation of the universe. Growth in knowledge must be joined by growth in grace. Spinoza pointed out the impact of education in the *Ethics:* "One mind, insofar as it understands, is an eternal mode of thinking, which is determined by another mode of thinking, and this again by another, and so on to infinity; so they all constitute at the same time the eternal and infinite intellect of God."

Education for citizenship is, therefore, not just an intellectual activity. It shapes the lives of boys and girls, men and women, and illuminates the ways of discharging their responsibilities toward their country and toward world society. Education is not limited to the process of communicating a given skill to successive generations. It also fills the world's spiritual vacuum by bringing understanding of the hearts and souls of men and of the divine laws governing the world. Are educational institutions responding to this need? Writing in the fourth century B.C. about the Peloponnesian War, Thucydides stressed the importance of "knowledge of the past as an aid to the interpretations of the future, which in the course of human things must resemble if it does not reflect it." In these times of genuine crisis for institutions of higher learning, much can be learned from recapitulation of educational changes in other countries during this century.

The Monolithic Character of Totalitarian Education

The appearance of Soviet Sputniks in the middle of this century was a great blow to our national pride. The national reappraisal that ensued plunged us into panic, accompanied by an exaggerated upgrading of our estimates of Russian education, training, and achievements. Our former state of blind confidence almost turned into an inferiority complex when we awoke suddenly to the fact that our mortal rival had taken the lead in an area in which we liked to think we excelled—science and technology. Our image of Russians altered radically. Formerly we had pictured Russians as bearded, backward peasants; in the panic brought on by the Sputniks, they emerged as the world's educational leaders, with superior methods of training and preparation. The revelations concerning Soviet educational advances caused a dangerous swing in the pendulum of public opinion to the opposite extreme—just short of admiration for the efficiency of a Communist dictatorship. In this admiration, we overlooked the fact that the educational system that exists in Soviet Russia is an admission of the defeat of Communist ideas of education, rather than an evidence of their success.

Immediately following the Revolution in Russia, the Soviet schools tried to toss overboard the "capitalist" educational system. The academic and disciplinary responsibility was vested in the hands of councils of pupils; marks, examinations, and the teacher's authority were abolished as an absurdity of capitalist "domination"; teaching by subjects was replaced by crude and dogmatic indoctrination along Marxist lines. The ruling clique, which became the new and merciless exploiting class, gripped control and superintendence over education to wage war on mental concentration. An educated man was dangerous; he could question or protest against slavery, against the horrors and absurdities of the clique that ruled through an army of highly paid secret police.

The immediate results of the Communist educational philosophy are now well-known: economic disorder, state-planned starvation in concentration camps, and a continued search for scapegoats. All these measures created a lack of skills. Well-trained technicians, specialists, and scientists became scarce in the Soviet Union. In the 1930s, in order to create minds capable of dealing with the growing economic domestic problems and to build a military machine, Soviet Russia abandoned the Communist educational principles and returned to the conservative educational methods of their hated capitalist enemy. The switch was simple. The old rigid educational system was again adopted; consequently, marks, examinations, the authority of the teacher, and even the same stern uniforms for school children that date from the time of Catherine the Great were restored. Mandatory job assignments followed graduation. Only a few top-ranking graduates had the privilege of choosing their place of work.

The Marxian goal of a "classless society" without "inequalities of wealth" was forgotten and the highest material rewards were offered for study and mental achievement. The only "contribution" made by the ruling class (the members of the Communist party) was the transformation of the schools, all the way from the elementary grades to the most advanced studies, into agencies for state training which closely resemble military agencies of training and mobilization. While education should concentrate on a fully developed human being, the motivating force of Soviet education is to produce a commodity which will best advance their system and establish the U.S.S.R. as a dominant power in the world.

World conquest requires skilled people, and the study of science is the key to power. Languages are needed to expand Russian imperialism and to establish contacts throughout the world. As a state agency, the Soviet school offers pragmatic education with emphasis on immediate utility; it is an education of monolithic character, without the virtues of diversity or the values contributing to intellectual integrity and to the spiritual needs of the individual. This educational system abjures the goal of developing broadly cultured minds and creates instead a trend to replace human thought with a machine-like regimentation. Academic freedom, in the sense that it is practiced in the western world, is unknown.

According to *The New York Times*, the number of Soviet scientists has quadrupled in the past three decades. In 1978, the last year in which comparable statistics were available, there were some 828,100 scientists in the Soviet Union, compared with 595,000 in the United States. The Soviet Union is investing more of its resources in scientific research than any other nation on earth. Some 4 percent of the Soviet gross national product is spent on research, compared with about 3 percent in this country, and Soviet science supplies the Kremlin's needs in many fields, predominantly in the field of war. Eighty percent of the research in the Soviet Union is for military purposes. This scientific underpinning of Soviet military strength may affect the future balance of world power. (Malcome W. Browne, "Soviet Science Assessed as Flawed but Powerful," *The New York Times*, May 20, 1980, p. C 1.)

Experts in the scientific field agree that the average Soviet scientist receives an education restricted to his specialty. He is denied access to foreign journals and books, and receives only the technical periodicals published abroad which pass the censor's test. The secret police surrounds and watches the Soviet scientists who attend conferences abroad. By sacrificing his freedom to the state, the Soviet scientist sacrifices also his perception of the wider implications of his work. The price of this sacrifice is a dullness that results from the fact that the state offers no other opportunity for creativity than that which the state itself sponsors. Such creativity has only two goals: the enhancement of military strength and of international prestige.

In totalitarian countries, youth are under the careful guard of the police state and are an integral part of its mechanism. They are taken to meetings, to clubs, to lectures, because only from these "pure sources" can they derive a knowledge of life. A citizen starts with faith in the party or dictator in power and must follow it to the end. With such "training," the future defenders of the regime become "adjusted" so as not to swerve from the pathway marked out for them. They lose the personal feeling of direction and meaning of life, and their emotions may become similar to the one described by Lord Byron in *The Prisoner of Chillon:*

> My very chains and I grew friends,
> So much a long communion tends
> To make us what we are:—even I
> Regain'd my freedom with a sigh.

Pasternak refers to this kind of Soviet "life adjustment" in his novel, *Dr. Zhivago,* as he described Russia after World War I: ". . . The main misfortune, the root of all the evil to come, was the loss of confidence in the value of one's own opinion. People imagined that it was out of date to follow their own moral sense, that they must all sing in chorus, and live by other people's notions, notions that were crammed down everybody's throat." (Boris Pasternak, *Dr. Zhivago,* Pantheon Books, 1958, p. 404.)

Such evils are not limited to the U.S.S.R., but occur in other totalitarian communist countries as well. In China the policies of Mao Tse-Tung emphasized adherence to the rigid political line of the party with contempt for intellectual achievement and distrust of intellectuals. The so-called Cultural Revolution which took place in Mao's declining years was marked by burning books, by humiliating and beating up professors, and by replacing the academic curricula by manual labor and indoctrination through "political studies."

After ten years of imposed ignorance and the destruction of a generation of educated persons, we can now witness a return to strictly academic standards in China. There are presently about one million students in Chinese institutions of higher education. This figure represents only one percent of the college-age population of the country, compared with almost 50 percent in the United States, where approximately eleven million students are enrolled in institutions of higher learning. Chinese authorities plan to triple the number of university students by 1990. The universities are also trying to reverse the trend of putting heavy emphasis on narrow specialization, which was adopted from the Soviet Union after the Communist takeover. During this period, research and development have been neglected and separated from teaching functions. The new curricula now being adopted include basic sciences, foreign languages, management, and humanistic culture.

After the period of anarchy in the system of higher education—a product of the revolution of 1949 and the Cultural Revolution of 1966-1979—the universities are now reintroducing the academic degrees which were abolished by the Cultural Revolution as much resented marks of superiority. Examinations have been reinstated and only the most gifted students are admitted to China's universities. Although some tendencies to hobble the educational process with radical leftish sloganism remain, the Chinese educational system is once again geared to produce competence rather than political orthodoxy. (See Barry Kramer, "China's Educational

Revolution," *The Wall Street Journal*, November 27, 1979, p. 24; and Martin and Adam Meyerson, "Reviving China's Universities," *The Wall Street Journal*, September 23, 1980, p. 26.)

Life Adjustment

A different type of life adjustment has been proclaimed in the United States as a goal of education. This trend in American schools, which stresses method over subject matter, is known as "progressive education" or "learning by doing." The so-called traditionalists believe that this trend is belligerently anti-intellectual. The "progressives," also called "educationalists" or followers of the "Whole Child" doctrine, tell us that their method favoring student-centered rather than subject-centered approaches is the best in the world. When the gap of controversy is so wide, there is always the danger that the facts and estimates concerning our education will fail to break through the crust of consciousness of the American public.

The fact remains that we have witnessed a great revolution in our educational philosophy. From Jefferson's highly selective educational program, which provided that only 20 percent of the best minds should be "raked from the rubbish" annually, we entered into a period during which the existence of differences between the abilities of individuals was not acknowledged. Neither was the aristocracy of subjects acknowledged. Mathematics and mechanics, art and agriculture, history and homemaking all became peers. Scholastic attainment was replaced with scholastic sameness or "togetherness." "What to teach" was replaced by "how to teach"; pragmatic skills replaced intellectual skills—the subject matter of traditional academic disciplines. To require or reward superior intellectual accomplishments or competence was proclaimed to be undemocratic.

Christian ethics, which, as I pointed out in this forum in my lectures last year, is a part of the common law and of our moral standards ("Dogmas and Moral Values," *The Third Way,* The Andrew R. Cecil Lectures on Moral Values in a Free Society, Volume I, The University of Texas at Dallas, 1980, pp. 25-27), does not acknowledge the existence of "rubbish," and proclaims the sacredness of all useful work which serves human needs. At the same time, it provides creative genius with full opportunity of expression and, thus, places before men the vision of man's greatness. In the parable of the talents, the man traveling into a far country gives his servants five, two, and one talent, "to every man according to his several ability" (Matthew 25:15). All men should have equal opportunities, but all men are not created with equal ability.

All men are born to equal political and civil rights. These rights do not require an egalitarianism offering only mediocrity. The assumption that all men are born with equal powers and faculties is, as John Adams declared, "a gross fraud." The damages caused by egalitarianism are extremely high: students of great ability are deprived of the opportunities to develop their talents; the academic curricula are diluted with proliferating nonintellectual courses; entrance and graduation requirements are weakened or abolished and grades inflated; authority at school and at home collapses; and moral standards, which safeguard society against cultural degeneration and sterility, are rejected.

The program of "life adjustments" offered by "progressive" education judges life in terms of abstract formulas. The followers of this program believe in an egalitarian, productive, and happy society without the help of eternal values by which our moral standards can be measured and compared across time. The idea of "adjustment" deprived of supporting moral force soon deteriorates into the contention that the purpose of "life adjustment" is to educate people to conform to the social conditions surrounding them. In this sense, Jesus, the early Christians, the founding fathers of this country, and the greatest men in history were obviously "maladjusted." Their lives were full of frictions and conflicts with their environment.

Were pain, anxiety, self-sacrifice, crucifixion, and death in the arena of the Roman circus the experiences of "maladjusted" persons? The pioneer circuit riders in this country were undoubtedly "maladjusted" to their environment of gambling, quarreling, and fighting, characteristic of the American frontier. When questioned in a 1976 BBC interview about Bertrand Russell's slogan, "Better red than dead," Alexander Solzhenitsyn said: "In this terrible expression of Bertrand Russell, there is an absence of all moral criteria. Looked at from a short distance this would allow one to maneuver and to continue to enjoy life; but from a long-term view, it will undoubtedly destroy those people who think like that." (*The Listener*, March 4, 1976, p. 261.)

Chief Justice Charles Evans Hughes, in his lectures at Yale in 1910 describing the virtues of citizenship, said, "No one can properly discharge his duties as a citizen who simply has a good-natured feeling towards all . . ." The first duty of a citizen is allegiance to the community and, therefore, he "must learn to make his personal decisions, as well as to define his public attitude, in light of the interests of the community, and not simply with respect to the opportunities for individual gain. No allurement of high salary or of social advantage, no promise of assistance to obtain public office, should be permitted to obscure [one's] duty of absolute loyalty to the public interest."

The European Ivory Tower

There are those who, in reaction to the abuses of progressive education, advocate the complete adoption of an educational standard patterned after the prewar European educational system, with its selectiveness, its sharp division between academic and vocational subjects, and its demands for concentrated efforts in such subjects as mathematics, sciences, foreign languages, history and philosophy. But did this educational system pass the crucial tests of citizenship? During the prewar period, graduates of European universities outnumbered all others in Nobel Prize winners in the fields of physics and chemistry, but the same universities faced a most tragic accusation: They failed to recognize their obligation to society. The universities excelled in detailed preparation for a profession, but did not even attempt to come to grips with the vital issues which were changing the destiny of nations, if not the course of the world's history.

The capitulation in prewar Germany of the apostles of universal culture and universal science and the courage of the church to defy the state was pointed out by Reinhold Niebuhr:

> The university was the pride of Germany; and the

> German church was more or less moribund. Yet the former has allowed its universal culture to be corrupted by the state while the latter has fought valiantly against such corruption. The culture of the university sought universal truth through the genius of the wise man; and forgot that the wise man is also a sinner, whose interest, passion and cowardice may corrupt the truth! (Reinhold Niebuhr, *Beyond Tragedy,* Charles Scribner's Sons, New York, 1937, p. 284.)

The mundane perspective of prewar European education and its trust in science channeled it into avenues of separation from life. The European universities hoped that the lights in the laboratories would continue to burn while the darkness of oppression surrounded their ivory towers; that the walls of the classrooms would be soundproof against the sirens of the secret police cars and groans of tortured prisoners. They forgot the classic remark attributed to Solon who, when asked how justice could be made secure in Athens, replied, "If those who are not injured feel as indignant as those who are."

With the growing emphasis on technology in this country, we have to be aware of the danger to education for citizenship described by Dr. Henry P. Van Dusen as "The typical American's glorification of the individual, his disdain of the past, his trust in science as mankind's Messiah, his inveterate optimism, his unchallengeable certitude of the fated prosperity and progress of his own nation, his estimate of the true values of life, his delight in gadgets and techniques, his religious unconcern, above all his unshaken confidence in man's power to know and to do—in brief, his this-worldly perspective." (Henry P. Van Dusen, *God in Education,* New York,

Charles Scribner's Sons, 1951, p. 50.) Knowledge and trained skill alone can put blinders on us, blinders that cover the sight of the central fact of human existence and exhaust the purpose of life in higher profits, higher wages, or shorter working weeks. Is this kind of hedonism the purpose of life? Does the greatness of a nation lie in its high standard of living or in its high standard of life?

Both "life adjustment" and "separation from life" systems of education lack the genuine value of relating education to high standards of life. Horace Mann in his address in Boston in 1842 stressed the need of intermingling the principles of science with principles of morality. "The multiplication tables," he said, "should not have been more familiar, nor more frequently applied, than the rule, to do to others as we would that they should do unto us." The question whether the impact of technological changes will be for good or evil is actually a moral question. Recognition of eternal values is essential to the implementation of moral principles, if not to their very existence. The values to be instilled in our young by education for citizenship include faith in the dignity of every individual, honor, duty, belief in the work ethic, loyalty, and patriotism. "By wisdom a house is built, and by understanding it is established" (Proverbs 24:3). The aim of education for citizenship must not be "life adjustment," not "separation from life," but growth—growth in the understanding of life.

The sciences do not formulate moral goals, they do not create a philosophy of life, they do not provide the final answer to mankind's problems. Scientific laws describe natural events in terms of cause and effect but do not explain the purposeful act of Creation of the universe by the Master of Planning. Aristotle, who in his *Nicomachean Ethics* wrote that ethics is a branch of politics and that education in morality should be the function of the state, also tried to reach for something beyond human qualities. Even as he wrote that "what is good for a nation or city has a higher, diviner quality" and that the life of the intellect is the best and the most satisfying to man, he added, "Such a life will be too high for *human* attainment. It will not be lived by us in our merely human capacity but in virtue of something divine within us . . ." (*The Ethics of Aristotle,* tr. J.A.K. Thomson, Allen & Unwin, 1953, pp. 15, 275.)

Only when knowledge is used for the growth of persons is a partnership formed between mind and soul. Such a partnership is an evidence of maturity. Spiritual enlightenment enables mental growth, guides the reason's efforts in finding purpose to the creation of the universe. Knowledge combined with moral values is the only force capable of guiding individuals and nations into the social application of conscience, which calls for love and service to fellowman. The union of "truth and love" forms a partnership of mind and soul. Growth in understanding of life calls not only for knowledge of values but also for commitment to them, commitment defined by Cardozo as "submergence of self in pursuit of ideals."

Changing Trends in Education

Each environment, each chapter in the history of civilization, each trend in art or literature has a climate differing in character. When we read in the Old Testament, we can sense a different atmosphere from that of the New Testament. Socrates, Plato, and Aristotle created a climate conducive to the acquisition of knowledge and to identifying virtue with intelligence, wisdom, and understanding of life's meaning. Two millenia later, Kant startled the world with a new metaphysical system and idealism calling for a new order of democracy and liberty everywhere.

What is the atmosphere, the environment that will tell us of the attitude and character of our universities and colleges? Whether our age will be called the era of "Watergate" or a "New Consciousness," of "Human Rights," or of "Restlessness," history will record that educational institutions were faced with the challenge of fulfilling their social responsibility by undergirding our communities with the strength that derives from educated men and women. What part do educational institutions perform in meeting this challenge for the spiritual and economic well-being of our nation, our communities, and the individual?

After the Civil War, private two-year schools experienced strong growth, with the church assuming the responsibility to meet the needs resulting from the breakdown of the educational system. The church became the schoolmaster of the South. In 1872, Dr. Thomas O. Sumners, editor of the *Nashville Christian Advocate,* wrote that three of the great Protestant communions—Baptist, Methodist, and Presbyterian—could educate all the children in the South. Other church leaders at this time predicted that the church would have a school wherever the Gospel is preached.

Presently, however, there is an undeniable shift in enrollment in institutions of higher learning to tax-supported schools. At the beginning of this century, 80 percent of all students were in private and church-related colleges and universities, and only 20 percent in tax-supported institutions. It is estimated that this figure will be reversed before the end of the century.

Many private colleges today are nondenominational or completely secular in nature. What they often have in common with the church-related colleges is that both are often rooted in Christian tradition. This tradition pervades the background and in varying degrees influences the character of private universities and colleges that are no longer church-related. Since today the approach to religion in these institutions differs so widely, in discussing the implications of the shift of enrollment to tax-supported institutions we shall limit our comments about private colleges and universities to those which are explicitly church-related. The Christian college not only has a religious program, it is a religious program. This distinction between *having* and *being* a religious program gives the reason for the existence of Christian institutions of higher learning.

State or municipal tax-supported institutions are not allowed to make comprehensive efforts to enhance the influence of religion on their campuses. They have courses in the history and theory of religion, but they lack the fundamental commitment and motivation that should pervade the Christian campus and make Christian faith relevant to any courses and programs offered on the campus. To be effective, religious education must have such relevance, and not consist of pious but impractical religious pronouncements or formulas that have no meaning to those whom they are addressed. Such an educational program must not, however, abdicate its responsibility to the real world, nor attempt to dictate doctrinaire solutions.

In church-related colleges, since religion covers a wide range of beliefs and commitments, it is natural that controversies arise about whether certain activities are peripheral or whether they constitute the very core of the college's being. The Religious Emphasis Week, for instance, is disappearing from our major university campuses. Some may believe that the passing of this traditional event is an evidence of the decline of religious activities on our campuses. Others may argue that one week in a year cannot take the place of long-term commitment on the part of the church and that the demise of the Religious Emphasis Week witnesses rather to the increasing seriousness with which the church is taking its task to be of service to the life of the university.

There are those who strongly believe that frequent and regular attendance at the service in college chapel is required to demonstrate the nature of the Christian college, which calls for fellowship of both prayer and study. Others see in the conventional uses of the chapel service an oversimplification of the relationship between faith and higher education and point out the danger of forms becoming more important than substance.

The Christian college should serve as a forum for controversies involving religious issues. Such discussions lead to understanding that the college does not automatically become Christian by conducting a Religious Emphasis Week, building a chapel, or offering a number of religious courses. Structures and strategies of the campus ministry should be open to modification and change, be versatile and flexible, but always be directed toward the creation of an atmosphere of Christian concern that combines integrity of scholarship with love expressed in personal commitment, self-control, and acceptance of responsibility.

The church-related college is the Church in education, in learning. Worship is the ground and reason for the college's existence only when combined with great, effective teaching. Intelligent Christian teaching must resist the danger of anti-intellectual pressure exercised by those who, in their lack of mature faith, try to shelter the students from the "modern" world. It must motivate the students to search for the truth, to find through creative thinking the purpose of life, and to discover the meaningfulness of the holy faith.

The support of church institutions of higher learning may depend upon ascertaining that the Christian college in its search for federal funding does not abdicate its responsibility to perform its duties in accordance with its fundamental commitment to studies that lead to understanding God's laws and discovery of God's truth. Supporters of Christian education may justly ask whether the church-related institution of higher learning performs its academic duties in the light of the Christian message or whether, in practice, it disassociates from the Christian basis on which it has been built.

Common Responsibility

The separation of church and state, the "wall of separation" concept under the Establishment Clause, does not permit public institutions to inculcate religious tenets or precepts in their students, but this does not mean that their students should not be made aware of the impact of moral standards offered by religion on our society. The recognition that religion is not solely a sectarian discipline, since it is concerned with human rights and the dignity of every individual, is the common responsibility of public as well as of private academic institutions. Thomas Jefferson outlined the necessity for all citizens to be aware of the questions raised by religious concern and of the various answers proposed for them:

> The relations which exist between man and his Maker, and the duties resulting from those relations, are the most interesting and important to every human being, and the most incumbent on his study and investigation. The want of instruction in the various creeds of religious faith existing among our citizens presents, therefore, a chasm in a general institution of the useful sciences.

The first and most immediate purpose of the First Amendment rested on the belief that a union of government and religion tends to destroy government and degrade religion. The separation of church and state does not imply, however, that the state institution should be contemptuous of the commitment that calls for adherence to Christians' concepts of morality. Supreme Courts in various states have taken the position that Christian morality is the ethical code of the majority of the citizens furnishing "the purest system of morality, the firmest auxiliary, and only stable support of all human laws." (*Updegraph v. Commonwealth*, [1824] 11 Serg.§ R[Pa.] 394. See also for similar positions *State v. Chandler*, [1839] 2 Harr. [Del.] 533, and *People v. Ruggles*, [1811] 8 Johns. R [N.Y.] 290, 5 Am. Dec. 335.) The Supreme Court of the United States has held that the Bill of Rights recognizes "that in the domain of conscience there is a moral power higher than the State." (*Girouard v. United States*, 328 U.S. 61, 68 [1946].) The courts refer not to religion in its totality, but to the Christian moral code which our law has adopted, recognizes, and embodies.

In more recent times the Supreme Court took the position that the state and religion are not required to be "aliens to each other—hostile, suspicious, and even unfriendly." It went on to say that "When the state encourages religious instruction or cooperates with religious authorities by adjusting the schedule of public events to sectarian needs, it follows the best of our traditions" and that "we find no constitutional requirement which makes it necessary for government to be hostile to religion and to throw its weight against efforts to widen the effective scope of religious influence." The Court gave specific recognition to the proposition that we "are a religious people whose institutions presuppose a Supreme Being." (*Zorach v. Clauson*, 343 U.S. 313-14 [1952].) The courts have also recognized that the Bible contains matters of great historical and literary value, as well as much moral instruction which is not in any sense sectarian. (68 Am. Jur. 2d 293.) In *Engel v. Vitale* (370 U.S. 421, 434 [1962]), the Court said: "The history of man is inseparable from the history of religions. . . . And since the beginning of that history many people have devoutly believed that 'More things are wrought by prayer than this world dreams of.'"

The separation of church and state, under a democratic form of government, does not mean that the state should be the central agency of power and that the only source of absolute standards of right and wrong is in fact the state. By the same token the church should not be the central agency of power. The totalitarian church is as dangerous as the totalitarian state. Under totalitarianism, the dictator's couriers—the members of the political party in power, the state agencies, and the press—offer security to their country by proclaiming the infallibility of the dictator and by deifying him. In their servility, they persuade citizens to praise if not glorify Hitler for revealing to them their racial superiority, Stalin for purging the "traitors," Khrushchev for crushing the revolution in Hungary, Brezhnev for invading Czechoslovakia or Afghanistan, or Khomeini for seizing the American embassy and holding American hostages.

Jeremiah warned against the false prophets who offer such security to their people: "They say still unto them that despise me, the Lord hath said, Ye shall have peace; and they say unto every one that walked after the imagination of his own heart, No evil shall come upon you" (Jeremiah 23:17). The false prophets defy God's laws of life, which call for love, justice, and legality, and Jeremiah, in his great concern over this betrayal of God's laws, expresses his distress: "Mine heart within me is broken because of the prophets; all my bones shake" (23:9).

Education for citizenship should foster freedom by pointing out the dangers of freeing the state to become its own god. The public confessions, forced by terror, to crimes never committed by political dissenters in communist countries remind us of the vivid story of the four hundred prophets in the first book of Kings. When Ahab, the King of Israel, asked Jehoshaphat, the King of Judah, to join him in a war against Ramoth-gilead, he gathered four hundred prophets who were attached to his court, and they unanimously delivered the prophetic verdict, "The Lord will deliver Ramoth-gilead into the hand of the king" (22:6). Only the prophet Micaiah, when asked by messengers to maintain the unanimity of the four hundred prophets, replied, "As the Lord liveth, what the Lord saith unto me, that will I speak" (22:14). When he painted the picture of the disaster which could be caused by the proposed war, the King of Israel banished him to prison.

The divinization of the state substitutes absolute nothingness for an absolute, fundamental conception of values. Arthur Koestler makes this point in his novel, *Darkness at Noon,* when he has his character Rubashov say in his manipulated confession:

> If I ask myself to-day, "For what am I dying?" I am confronted by absolute nothingness. There is nothing for which one could die, if one died without having repented and unreconciled with the Party and the Movement. Therefore, on the threshold of my last hour, I bend my knees to the country, to the masses and to the whole people. The political masquerade, the mummery of discussions and conspiracy are over. We were politically dead long before the Citizen Prosecutor demanded our heads. Woe unto the defeated, whom history treads into the dust." (Koestler, *Darkness at Noon,* Macmillan, 1941, p. 251.)

Throughout the history of mankind there has been an ongoing search for absolute moral values, for the absolute laws which Cicero described as "*Lex ad quam non eruditi sumus sed nati sumus* "—the laws to which we are born and not trained. Hammurabi, Moses, Confucius, the Greek philosophers, the Roman jurists and statesmen, the philosophers and scientists who molded our modern civilization—they all looked for fundamental moral values imbedded in all phases of the development of civilization, whether they like Aristotle considered that "the state or political community . . . is the highest good of all" or like St. Augustine, who by identifying the church with the kingdom of God and by claiming divinity for this human institution, saw the church as the highest active force for social justice.

Public educational institutions cannot divorce themselves from the fact that Christianity has entered and influenced, more or less, all our institutions, customs, and relations, as well as all our individual modes of thinking and acting. "It is involved in our social nature, that even those among us who reject Christianity, cannot possibly get clear of its influence, or reject those sentiments, customs and principles which it has spread among the people, so that, like the air we breathe, they have become the common stock of the whole country, and essential elements of its life." (*Mohney v. Cook*, 26 Pa. 342 [1855].)

Among the traditions of our nation in which religion has become intertwined with government are chaplains in both Houses of Congress, chaplains in all branches of the Armed Forces, compulsory chapel at the military service academies, the use of the Bible for oaths, religious proclamations by the President, the reference to God on coins and in the pledge of allegiance, exemption of religious organizations from taxation, and deduction of religious donations for income tax purposes.

The common responsibility of public and private academic institutions—the inquiring conscience of society—is to provide the student with a conception of what it means to be a free man and with stable standards of moral judgment. No educational institution should become a political instrument or the obliging servant of any political or economic group. Alongside intellectual discipline and scientific study, it has to fulfill the express purpose of building character upon the foundation of moral principles. Its sacred task is to combine the love of learning with the citizen's allegiance to his community. The concern for virtues and spiritual values is the very core of the existence of academic institutions whether public, private, or church-related. They are committed to develop persons of strong moral character who would serve their fellowman. They are committed to share convictions strongly rooted in their heritage of leadership that comes from within the institution and is reflected in the entire pattern of learning and campus life.

Without the general direction of the moral code calling for service to our fellowman, human society becomes aimless and meaningless, and pursuit of pleasure that weakens its spiritual fiber takes the place of the pursuit of happiness guaranteed by the Declaration of Independence. A society in which rights to personal gratification and well-being are stressed without correlating them with obligations to one's fellowman and one's country cannot survive.

In order to avoid generalities, we would like to cite a few examples of how knowledge supplemented by moral principles creates a climate out of which commitment to service may emerge in such varied disciplines as medicine, law, economics, and the sciences. Moral and spiritual fiber may not substitute for medical skill, but it may induce students of medicine to give their lives on the altar of service to mankind in search of means for delivering man from the sufferings that beset him. Albert Schweitzer pointed out that his determination to become a medical missionary stemmed from the growing understanding within himself of Jesus' message that we must not treat our lives as being for ourselves alone and that "whoever is spared personal pain must feel himself called to help in diminishing the pain of others." (*Out of My Life and Thought*, Henry Holt, 1933, pp. 81-82.)

In the law schools, in addition to the study of man-made statutes, rules, court decisions, and administrative regulations, there should be a constant search for moral order. In the words of Reinhold Niebuhr, "The cure for modern lawlessness is not more emphasis upon law or efforts to define specific laws more sharply. The cure for modern lawlessness is to bring the idolatry and self-worship of all men and nations under divine judgement..." (*Man's Disorder and God's Design*, Amsterdam Assembly Series, Volume III, Harper Brothers, p. 27.) The principles found in Leviticus, "In righteousness shall you judge your neighbor" (19:15), and expressed by Paul, "Love cannot wrong a neighbor; therefore, the whole law is summed up in love" (Romans 13:10), constitute the very framework of the administration of justice.

Man's giant strides in knowledge and control of his natural environment, his trust and dependence on the power of science also put in his hands the power of annihilation of the human race. It is the responsibility of education for citizenship to inspire an apathetic world and to renew the affirmation of the rule of law, the only instrument strong enough to forestall this annihilation. No society can endure without order and due process (Romans 13:1-7). Respect for the rule of law creates no conflict with the right of legal redress and of dissent. The integrity of our administration of justice depends upon its vivid response to warranted complaints of injustice and inequity. The sufferings of the early Christians are constant reminders of the importance of the rights of free speech and peaceful assembly.

Nor can an educated citizen be complacent in the face of economic exploitations and inequalities of wealth when multitudes are sick of poverty and hunger. In socialistic countries, the attempts to eliminate inequalities in wealth result in making everyone poor. This is not the equality we seek. Inequalities that do not endanger the well-being of society, and do not tend to destroy fellowship, must be accepted, provided that every citizen has the right to equal opportunities through equal access to education and employment.

There is a need for the incentive and initiative of every citizen who has not only the right but also the obligation to work, and through work to serve the community. Work should minister to the worker's spiritual welfare as well as to the community's welfare. There is no Christian physics, mathematics, or botany. As Harold C. Case, President of Boston University, has pointed out, "When a Christian teacher imparts his knowledge of mathematics or botany to his student, his faith adds overtones so that the same subject matter has an inspiring glow and deeper meaning." This faith enhances what the French philosopher Jean-Jacques Rousseau observes—the inner nobility of man.

Education for World Citizenship

In the first series of lectures on Moral Values in a Free Society, I defined a Christian world citizen as a "patriot who exerts himself to promote the welfare of his country, ready to defend it against open or subversive aggression, but who, at the same time, is concerned about the welfare of other nations and with compassion is ready to share his fellowman's destiny." (Cecil, *The Third Way*, p. 131.)

In the Old Testament, the early Hebrews claimed a peculiar relationship to God as his chosen people. But the prophets saw God's love as transcending national boundaries and his concern as extending to the destinies of other peoples besides his own. Amos asks: "Are ye not as children of the Ethiopians unto me, children of Israel? saith the Lord. Have not I brought up Israel out of the land of Egypt? and the Philistines from Caphtor, and the Syrians from Kir?" (Amos 9:7).

The Hebrews are not the only nation who have needed such reminders. We too, like other nations, have sometimes subscribed to the unconscious ideal of a national god while pretending to call upon and worship the eternal and universal God. In times of war, men in opposing camps characteristically invoke the aid of "their" God, and troops are sent into the battlefield in the belief that God is "on their side." During the time of our own Civil War, Lincoln noted this anomaly, saying of the North and South that "Both read the same Bible and pray to the same God, and each invokes his aid against the other. The prayers of both could not be answered." And again in his Second Inaugural Address he noted, "It seems strange that men should ask the assistance of God in wringing their bread from other men's toil."

The eternal and universal God is not an ally of any one nation engaged in battle. As Niebuhr pointed out, this is why in the first book of Chronicles God said to David, "thou shalt not build an house for my name, because thou hast been a man of war and hast shed blood. . . . Solomon thy son, he shall build my house and my courts . . ." (I Chronicles 28:3, 6, as quoted in Niebuhr, *Beyond Trag-*

edy, p. 48.) The true vision of the eternal and universal God leads in turn to a vision of sacred brotherhood, "with malice toward none, with charity toward all," and recognizes that the gospel passage "God so loved the *world* that he gave his only-begotten Son" (John 3:15) cannot be limited in its application to any one country or people.

Because of our obligations to our fellowmen throughout the world, an essential component of education for citizenship is training young people for service in underdeveloped areas throughout the world. It is vital that we demonstrate the principles of world citizenship by both word and deeds and that our interest in the well-being of people of underdeveloped nations be free from any design to exploit or oppress them or to seek any special privileges. To be effective in teaching the people living under subnormal conditions our know-how, its application in modern industry and agriculture, and how our scientific advancement might be used efficaciously—we must win the friendship and confidence of the peoples of underdeveloped areas.

How can we win the confidence of the peoples of underdeveloped areas? First, we must recognize the meaning and values of *patience.* In our program for underdeveloped countries we must be prepared for rocky enterprises. With technological backwardness in many countries are preserved archaic land relations and, what is worse, ignorance and superstition. The trust in progress will come when people become convinced that someone is trying to share with them the God-given human rights to which they are entitled.

Second, the knowledge of the native language has fundamental implications in the course of human relations. In the sixteenth century the British philosopher

Francis Bacon wrote, "He that travelleth into a country before he has some entrance into the language, goeth to school, and not to travel." Friendship is a "plant of slow growth," and the knowledge of the language of our neighbors gives the great opportunity to find an accord in our common affairs and to eliminate the seeds of suspicion in the minds of the natives of the underdeveloped countries. The friendliness which we try to offer is often seriously discounted by the incorrect usage or non-usage of their language. Training in foreign languages has been proved to break down the communication barrier and to lead to understanding and respect of the culture and customs of the native world.

The exclusiveness of foreigners' residential "colonies" or enclaves can also in no way be considered as a contribution to our friendship with the peoples of underdeveloped countries. Representatives of industrialized countries living abroad often confine their social contacts mostly to themselves. Such self-insulated walls exclude association with new friends, and this attitude is generally interpreted as egotism and wounds those sensitively searching for equality. The local citizens know that their countries are underdeveloped. Their recognition of this fact is one of the chief reasons why the way we deal with them attracts special attention. Their national, or merely human, pride is offended when we are indifferent to their traditions and customs. It is important that the foreign technician, businessman, or missionary take interest in the new culture in which he lives, reading books and magazines other than in his native language, making friends with others than those of his own cultural group.

Third, we must stress the meaning and value of modesty. The underdeveloped countries are areas in which income is very low and distribution of income results in fundamental injustices. The people under the prevailing system of oligarchy or dictatorship are not able to secure their necessities. We have therefore to remember that poverty breeds strife and that envy is a human passion which, according to La Rochefoucauld, is more irreconcilable than hatred. "Wrath is cruel, and anger is outrageous, but who is able to stand before envy?" (Proverbs 27:4).

We cannot expect our friends in underdeveloped areas to admire without envy our good fortune and our high standards of living. Confucius once wrote: "It is harder to be poor without murmuring than to be rich without arrogance." There is the undercurrent of hostility of the poor and hungry toward those who possess and enjoy abundance and plenty. The Spanish proverb says: "Quien ha criados ha enemigos no escusados" (he who has servants has unavoidable enemies).

Fourth, there is one more factor that should be taken into consideration. In underdeveloped countries we can find the economic power concentrated in the hands of a few, who live in luxury unknown even in the United States. They often use the campaign against the American engineer, businessman, or teacher, who lives much more comfortably than the starving miner or factory worker, as a handy way of diverting attention from domestic injustices. The "spirit" of this type of campaign explains the hostile attitude toward the foreigners in some of the underdeveloped countries. The truth is that in order to give a living example of world citizenship we cannot be complacent in the face of economic exploitation and inequalities of wealth when multitudes are sick and tired of poverty, famine, and hunger.

In spite of the opposition to "foreign millionaires," the people of the underdeveloped countries realize the work done for them not only in the field of religion, but in public health, social service, and education. Great care must be taken in recruiting the right type of personnel for such activities and in giving them special training in the culture and the needs of the areas to which they go. The sooner we carry out our task of helping the peoples of the underdeveloped areas, the better are the hopes for a free world. A large part of the unrest in the Third World results from an upsurge of the people who have long suffered in poverty and misrule.

Arnold J. Toynbee, one of the great twentieth-century historians, concluding his address on "Man at Work in God's World," delivered before the Church and Work Congress, stated:

> My first point is that Man's Work in God's World cannot be healthy or beneficent unless we consecrate it . . . My second point is that the price of consecration is the same as the price of liberty: it is eternal vigilance—and the exercise of this vigilance cannot be delegated by you and me to the public authorities, civil or ecclesiastical, for them to administer it for us vicariously. This is not feasible, because the place where Work is consecrated is not the impersonal field of relations between us which we call Society; the place where Work goes right or wrong is the soul of each individual human being . . ." (*Vital Speeches*, Volume XXII, No. 3, p. 96.)

The signers of the Declaration of Independence pledged their lives, fortunes, and sacred honor. "Sacred honor" is embodied in the conception of entire surrender to the will of God. Such surrender provides a spiritual force which will lend purpose to the task of efficient government and citizenship. Supported by this force, the emotionally and intellectually mature citizen will have the ability to relate his talents to continuing progress of the society in which he lives. "None of us lives to himself, and none of us dies to himself" (Romans 14:7).

ETHICS IN GOVERNMENT

by

Leon Jaworski

The Honorable Leon Jaworski

Mr. Jaworski received his LL.B. from Baylor University and his LL.M. from George Washington University. The recipient of fifteen honorary degrees, he has also been the president of the Houston Bar Association, the State Bar of Texas, the American Bar Association, and the American College of Trial Lawyers. He is a senior partner of the law firm Fulbright & Jaworski in Houston.

In 1973–74, Mr. Jaworski served as special prosecutor in the Watergate investigation, and in 1977–79 as special counsel to the Committee on Standards of Official Conduct of the United States House of Representatives in the investigation of South Korean influence in the United States. In addition, he has held five presidential appointments to various committees.

Mr. Jaworski has served as chairman of the board of trustees of The Southwestern Legal Foundation and as president of the Baylor Medical Foundation and the M.D. Anderson Foundation.

Among numerous other professional and civic awards, Mr. Jaworski has received the American Bar Association Gold Medal Award, the Courageous Advocacy Award from the American College of Trial Lawyers, and the Great Leaders Award from The Southwestern Legal Foundation. Each of these awards is the highest honor the organization can bestow.

Following service as a Colonel in the Judge Advocate General's Department during World War II, Mr. Jaworski acted as Chief of the War Crimes Trials Section of the United States Army in the European theater. He personally prosecuted the first major war crimes trials in that theater, and was awarded the Legion of Merit.

Mr. Jaworski has contributed many articles to legal journals, and is the author of After Fifteen Years *and* The Right and the Power.

ETHICS IN GOVERNMENT

by

Leon Jaworski

Lawyers have their code of professional responsibility which delineates acceptable ethical conduct and, we find, requires revision from time to time due to social advancements and changes in the conduct of human affairs. Doctors have their Hippocratic Oath in which the Greek physician Hippocrates embodies the pledge of the medical profession to mankind. Ministers of religion have long followed exacting standards of behavior among themselves as well as in ministering to parishioners. In more recent years there has been a growing trend to the maintenance of rules of ethical conduct among other professions and businesses as well.

There is no all-encompassing written code to delineate the conduct of governmental officials. There are government institutions and agencies which have formulated some written rules of ethical conduct and, as we shall later see, have committees and groups within their ranks designated to administer disciplinary action where ethical rules have been violated.

In our society, there may well exist a contrariety of views on what is ethical in some professional and business situations—even an uncertainty as to the relevance of an ethical principle to a particular problem. But I hold to the belief that there should not be drawn a fine line of demarcation in determining the ethical conduct of a public official. He (or she) knows the difference between right and wrong—otherwise the qualification to hold public office is lacking. And so knowing, it is incumbent on the official, in public affairs, to hold himself, as Caesar expected of his wife—above suspicion. It was Caesar, it is appropriate to add, who as early as 45 B.C. included among his reforms a high level of probity of his governors.

Thus in this lecture, I will not be dealing with fine-spun theories or hypotheses on the subject of ethics in public life. No ethician, I approach the subject as a pragmatist.

Most, if not all, dictionaries define "ethics," "ethical," and the like as "pertaining to right and wrong in conduct." Thus it is not uncommon to find provisions in some codes of ethics restating what is forbidden by civil and criminal law. As respects matters involving questioned conduct of public officials, almost invariably the inquiry relates to conduct criminally culpable. The House Ethics Committee as well as the Senate Ethics Committee of our Congress rarely deal with any inquiry not involving criminal wrongdoing.

In recent years, perhaps more than at any other time in this century, the spotlight has been thrown on unethical conduct in public office. Clearly this is true on the national level. Among recent publications dealing with this general topic is Sissela Bok's volume on *Lying: Moral Choice in Public and Private Life* (Pantheon). Her views and conclusions are put in these words:

> We live at a time when the harm done to trust can be seen first-hand. Confidence in public officials and in professionals has been seriously eroded.
>
> What role can the government play in such efforts? First, it can look to its own practices, to the very

> "climate" of its dealings with the public. It will take time and great effort to try to reverse the injuries to trust and to public life of the last decades.

And Steve Allen in his recent book, *Rip-Off* (Lyle Stuart), points to numerous wrongdoings in public office, some of which I am familiar with and will refer to in the comments that follow.

And finally I point to the very revealing book, *Gifts of Deceit*, by Robert Boettcher (Holt, Rinehart-Winston) which deals with the questionable conduct of members of Congress with representatives of the South Korean government.

Of central interest in understanding the problems of ethics in government as they exist today is to roll back the calendar a few years and examine the expanding circle of conditions that finally have produced the state of concern confronting us today.

In 1965 President Lyndon Johnson, recognizing the urgency of the nation's crime problem, established a Commission on Law Enforcement and Administration of Justice which was generally known as the President's Crime Commission. After much study, research, and the conducting of numerous hearings as well as many staff investigations, the Commission issued its report, "The Challenge of Crime in a Free Society." The report dealt with the full spectrum of crime in our country. It therefore included the subject of white collar crime and defined the "white collar" criminal. As a member of this class of criminal offenders, the report identified *"the legislator who peddles his influence and vote for private gain."* (Emphasis supplied.) It reviewed organized crime activities and pointed out that the neutralizing of local law enforcement "is central to organized crime's operations." It propounded the question, "What can the public do if no one investigates the investigators, and the political figures are neutralized by their alliance with organized crime?" It deplored "that it is impossible to determine how extensive the corruption of public officials by organized crime has been." It added that "we do know that there must be more vigilance against such corruption." This report was published in 1967.

In the years that followed, the observations of this report were largely ignored. Then came violence on the campus and violence in the streets. President Johnson appointed another commission known as the Violence Commission for the purpose of concentrating particularly on the causes of so much violence and how to cope with it. It was a happenstance that I served on both Commissions.

I well recall that as the work of the Violence Commission was in progress I received many communications from interested citizens, both young and old, who commented on our studies and labors. More common than any other communication was the inquiry of why more attention was not being paid to white collar crime—especially official misconduct—and why there was not more activity by way of combating this phase of crime. The question was not easy to answer. It seemed that at all levels of government law enforcement, officials were occupied with elements of crime that seemed to them more dangerous to society—crime that involved physical harm or loss of life—thus relegating white collar crime to the background.

Now it appears that there has been a reversal of thought in the significance of white collar crime and that there is a realization by at least some of our enforcement officials that this nonviolent category of crime is dangerously harmful to the welfare of our nation. And something dramatic has been done about it.

As this is being written (spring of 1980), we have been reading and hearing that the Federal Bureau of Investigation, under the direction of its head, William H. Webster, had been conducting an undercover investigation of public officials as a "sting" operation. We need not go into the history of "sting" operations and how they acquired this designation. Suffice it to say that traditionally these have been operations to garner evidence against criminals engaged in buying up stolen goods and other illicit operations difficult to combat without the use of undercover agents. This recent FBI investigation has touched a number of areas—the most dramatic and shocking of which involved the investigation of several members of Congress. How far-flung and how fully revealing this operation may actually have been may not be known for some time. But we know enough for us to have been jolted to a rude awakening of gross failures of methods and practices of the past.

Should the massive FBI investigation involving members of Congress have come as a surprise to us? In my view it was overdue.

A nationwide poll taken last year divulged an unexpected result. What is our greatest concern today? This was the question directed to each individual polled. Of course, as you would surmise—inflation was selected as the number one problem. But what you would not have surmised and what I think is appalling to all of us is that almost the same number—with only a very slight variance—pointed to corruption in government as being our greatest concern. And would you believe that crime and violence ran a poor third?

On the heels of this poll came a news release from the Justice Department announcing that more public officials were convicted across the country on federal corruption charges in 1977 and 1978 than ever before. The department's public integrity section released a report showing a steady rise in the number of federal, state, and local officials indicted on federal charges during the last nine years—from 63 in 1970 to 557 in 1978. It said that of the 2,622 cases brought during that period, juries have found the defendants guilty more than 75 percent of the time. Convictions have been obtained in 80 percent of the cases brought in the last two years, the department said. The figures for 1979 are not available to me at this time, but I am confident they correspond to the trend.

In the past four years in particular, there has been a rash of official misconduct on the part of members of Congress involving ill-gotten gain based on payroll irregularities, false expense accounts, improper receipt of funds, and other instances of so-called financial misconduct. There was scandal after scandal, with only one member being involved in some, and with several involved in others. Some of the findings made by the investigating committees were such as to justify the expulsion of the members involved, and in some instances no less than a suspension would have been appropriate. But in none was a sentence of this nature imposed. Instead, there were slaps on the wrist—like a reprimand. Even in the recent instance of Senator Herman Talmadge of Georgia, in which the Senate committee's findings were that the Senator had been guilty of "reprehensible" conduct in the misuse of government funds, the Senator was merely "denounced"—whatever that means. The Senators could not muster enough courage to "censure" their fellow Senator. So they coined a new word of purported punishment to spare their comrade from public rebuke on the floor of the Senate. The Senators, after ducking out, sent the file to the Department of Justice, which so far has done nothing. Apparently the Justice Department is nonplussed by the timid punishment imposed by the Senate. It is clear that this was a matter for the criminal courts from the beginning.

What I learned about congressional investigations was an eye opener, and when I completed my service as special counsel to the House Ethics Committee, I had no difficulty understanding the lack of public confidence in congressional investigations of improper conduct of its own members. The simple truth is that Congress has no business investigating alleged criminal conduct of its members, and the poor showing it has made in this regard constitutes one of its worst self-inflicted wounds.

That weak disciplinary action, tantamount to virtually no punishment, may be an encouragement rather than a deterrent to commission of wrongdoing is well illustrated by what happened in the case of a California congressman. In the South Korean investigation he was found to have accepted an unreported gift from Tongsun Park, the South Korean influence seeker. He was also found to have lied about this gift. Drastic punishment would have been appropriate, but instead of suspension or expulsion or even censure, he was given a meaningless reprimand. He must have scoffed at it.

The eventual result? He was brought back before the Ethics Committee of the House of Representatives—charged with having received and handled contributions illegally. This is precisely what happens when law enforcement is lax and ineffective.

I submit that the conclusion is justified that the laxity of Congress in instituting and conducting prompt, thorough, and impressive investigations of misconduct of its members, and the lackadaisical and detached attitude in inflicting appropriate punishment on guilty members, have contributed to increased misconduct of its members in recent years. Lately, the House has embarked on a new era. It supported its Ethics Committee in the recommendation that one of its members convicted of a bribery charge in ABSCAM be expelled.

Voter vigilance and perhaps even news media vigilance may have been a contributing factor to a failure properly to deal with the wrongdoing of some members of Congress. Two of the congressmen convicted of serious wrongdoing in the South Korean investigation were returned to office by California voters. Another found guilty of serious criminalities in the misuse of public funds was returned to office in Pennsylvania. Either the voters failed to inform themselves or lapsed into an attitude of indifference on the outcome of the election. It could be that the news media likewise failed in the performance of its duty. It would seem that if the media had effectively carried to the voters the findings of criminal wrongdoing of these individuals and of their lack of trustworthiness, the outcome of the elections may well have been different. But the more reasonable explanation for such a political debacle is that the voters were misled by the light and unimpressive treatment accorded these offenders by their fellow congressmen—and thought little of their wrongs.

It would be an interesting study to examine the voting records of congressmen in the *Congressional Record* to ascertain those who have been consistently inclined to deal out weak punishments—almost no punishments at all—to their fellow congressmen when found guilty of wrongdoing—criminal wrongdoing. This would be a useful exercise for enterprising members of the news media to pursue—and it could be highly revealing. Not always, but quite often, when a person winks at the commission of official misconduct, his own outlook on malfeasance in office could stand improvement. It became clear to me that during the course of the South Korean investigation there were some congressmen who were not in sympathy with the ultimate objectives of the inquiry and eventually joined in a movement to let the guilty off the hook with less than appropriate punishment.

Ironically, instead of saluting the FBI for its effective undercover work in investigating corruption in public office, a backlash of criticism is ensuing from some quarters which is difficult for me to rationalize. Instead of focusing on the sad plight of the vulnerability of public officials to bribery approaches, reactionaries are pointing to alleged dirty tactics. To catch a crook it is usually necessary to conduct undercover work involving stealth. It is not to be expected that any would accept money at high noon on the front steps of the Capitol.

Whether any of the legal barriers against entrapment were transgressed will be determined in due course of time. Let us assume that it is found that the technical defense of entrapment prevails. Where does that leave the public official who was so weak and so vulnerable to temptation as to let his influence be bought even under circumstances of artful enticement? His moral wrongs remain the same. He is unfit for public office, whether it be because of a corrupt heart or a weak spirit. It is high time, I submit, that we insist upon untarnished integrity in our officeholders and leave the legal niceties to the courtroom.

A public official should hold himself aloof from any conversations or dealings suggestive of attempts to corrupt the political process. He should not be a participant in discussions that taint his official conduct. He should insulate himself against any transaction or contact that has the appearance of wrongdoing. Once he follows this course, he will never have to fall back on the technical defense of entrapment. There are some factual situations that warrant the defense of "entrapment" in criminal prosecution. This involves a legal doctrine based more on wrongful enticement by enforcement officers than on innocent conduct of the accused. In my book, a public official, honest to the core, cannot be *morally* entrapped.

It is especially deplorable that in the public mind an entire institution of government becomes suspect because of the corrupt practices of some of its members. The good and faithful members of such a branch of our government deserve a better fate than to be collectively demeaned because of the wrongful conduct of a few. Many of them have been rendering dedicated service, some of whom are from our state. Therefore, it is to their interest, as well as to the public interest, that those who have been unfaithful to their public trust be weeded out and eliminated from public service and that those who seek to serve in the future be forewarned of the high degree of probity expected of them.

I am convinced that Congress should not meddle with investigations where criminal wrongdoing on the part of members of Congress is involved. Congress has proven itself to be a poor investigator—and even less qualified to sit as a tribunal considering appropriate punishment. I have no quarrel with Congress continuing to investigate matters that relate purely to a violation of its code of ethics, but I think that Congress by its past performance has forfeited its right to investigate criminal wrongdoing. The latter should be left to the enforcement officials who can apply the judicial process without the delay, interference, and handicaps that congressional investigations cause. The expulsion by the House to which I alluded earlier came not as a result of an investigation by the House, but after a conviction was obtained based on evidence gathered by the FBI.

Let me make it crystal clear that by these comments I am not prejudging the guilt of any individual associated with these accusations or who may be the target of any investigation. But the startling inferences and innuendos of recent weeks require full and effective action and no undue delays in the operation of the judicial process. In instances of conviction, appropriate punishment should be assessed, and in instances of innocence, the names of the accused should be cleared at the earliest practicable time. A prolonged, cumbersome, and perhaps dilatory congressional investigation is wholly unacceptable. Such a proceeding would only serve to interfere with and perhaps permanently handicap an effective eventual criminal prosecution.

It is difficult to conceive of anything more heinous in the category of white collar crime than a betrayal of the public trust. If such practices take root and spread in our institutions politic, an erosion in the foundations of our government is bound to follow.

I am purposely omitting any comment involving recent investigations of public officials in my state. The investigative and enforcement procedures and policies are different. There are no "in-house" investigations to delay or interfere with the work of law enforcement officials. As to the Texas charges, we can all look forward to thorough investigations and the application of due process of law.

This brings me to an aftermath to the present investigation suggested by some writers. I have been appalled to read that it is being conjectured that the result of the FBI investigations probably will be that there will be additional disenchantment of our voters; that it would result in "turning off" voters so as to keep many of them from the polls this fall. The aftermath should be just the opposite. It should bring about a renaissance in voting activity. It should encourage the disenchanted voter to know that meaningful investigations are pursued where suspicions exist. It should show the voter that measures are taken to assure honesty in office—that the upright have nothing to fear and that the weak and greedy should beware. For the citizen to abstain from exercising the high prerogative of expressing his views in the voting booth would be the severest blow that could be dealt to good government. This could cause the processes of government to fall by default into undesirable hands.

In 1831 there was a young man from France, accomplished in scholarship, philosophy, and statesmanship, who was sent by the French governnment to our country primarily to examine prisons and penitentiaries. He became intrigued by our system of government and its institutions and therefore devoted considerable time to analyzing life in America. On his return he wrote his classic *Democracy in America*, published in 1835 and again in 1840. This volume represented a wide-ranging study of the political and social institutions of the United States. Scholars have commented that the result of de Tocqueville's visit to America and the writings that followed brought forth not only "the greatest book ever written on America, but probably the greatest on any national polity and culture."

In summarizing what he found in our country, he said:

> I sought for the greatness and genius of America in her commodious harbors and her ample rivers, and it was not there.
>
> I sought for the greatness and genius of America in her fertile fields and boundless forests, and it was not there.
>
> I sought for the greatness and genius of America in her rich mines and her vast world commerce, and it was not there.
>
> I sought for the greatness and genius of America in her public school system and her institutions of learning, and it was not there.
>
> I sought for the greatness and genius of America in her democratic Congress and her matchless Constitution, and it was not there.

Then, after he paid tribute to the pulpits that were "aflame with righteousness," in ringing words he declared:

> America is great because America is good, and if America ever ceases to be good, America will cease to be great.

When de Tocqueville spoke of America being "good," what did he mean? The reasonable assumption is that he was using the word in connection with its usual definition.

"Good" when de Tocqueville used the word, and as well today, is defined as "something that satisfies or commends itself to the ethical consciousness or is conceived as fitting in the moral order of the universe." It is defined as the character of human beings or of their attitudes, motives, and actions that is morally praiseworthy.

Let's take a closer look at de Tocqueville's ultimate finding. Note that he did not attribute America's greatness to the power vested in the executive branch—not to the power lodged in the legislative branch—not in the authority and jurisdiction of the judiciary—not even, as you heard, in our "matchless Constitution." He regarded these as what they are—the processes and means whereby good government can be achieved. But these processes are all administered by human beings and are all subject to human error and frailty. He looked beyond the visible structure of government. He went deeper and took a look at the foundation on which the edifice was built. He saw in America a foundation of morality which led her to greatness and in light of this unmistakable truth he admonished the then-generation of Americans as well as generations to come that "if America ever ceases to be good—it will cease to be great."

As I was drafting this lecture, my thoughts turned to a recent visit to Independence Hall where the Declaration of Independence was signed, and eleven years later, after four months of debate, deliberation, study, and prayer, our Constitution was drafted. There were vast differences of opinions and a great contrariety of views permeating these extensive sessions of the Constitution, yet in the end dissents were largely resolved by an understanding approach to opposing views of the participants and the acceptance of sincereness and good faith on the part of all. The eventual result was a monumental document that has stood the test of time and has enabled us daily to enjoy the freedoms and the individual rights it guarantees.

To remind me—almost to haunt me—came the recollections of immortal words they penned—the pledge to each other of "our lives, our fortunes, and our sacred honor." Then I paused to wonder—are these just empty words to many of us today—or are they still as radiant, as inspirational, and as binding in our pursuits as they were to these great founders of freedom and seekers of justice? Do we still hold dear our "sacred honor"? What tortured my thinking was the unquestioned integrity of these patriots—their trustworthiness and guilelessness—as contrasted with the shams and deceits and corruptions perpetrated by some of their successors of modern times.

Still fresh on my mind is the sadness of seeing one of the great tragedies of modern history—men who once had fame in their hands sinking to infamy—all because eventually their goals were of the wrong dreams and aspirations. The teaching of right and wrong had been forgotten and little evils were permitted to grow into great evils—small sins to escalate into big sins. How did Alexander Pope put it? "Unblemished, let me live or die unknown. Give me an honest fame or give me none."

When drafting the Declaration of Independence, Thomas Jefferson devoted much time to research of historical backgrounds and experiences of other nations. Undoubtedly, he devoted much study and thought to what produced greatness in a nation—and also what caused a nation to fall. In addition to writing the drafted words of the Declaration of Independence, he voiced his beliefs and philosophies on the structure and mechanism of a truly good environment—one that served well in time of plenty as well as in time of need. He summed up his findings and conclusions with this statement: "The whole art of government consists in the art of being honest." This is a rather plain and simple statement, but its implications are far-reaching. Jefferson was talking about conduct in office based on forthrightness and not guilefulness; uprightness and not deceit; integrity and not double-dealing. He was speaking of fidelity to duty and not caprice; he meant undiluted truthfulness and not half truths; he referred to statesmanship and not demagoguery; he had in mind unvarnished patriotism and love of country—not self-service and avarice. And finally, he was alluding to wholehearted service to one's country and its people and not to an obligation or allegiance to special groups or interests.

It should not be necessary to interpolate that Jefferson was not saying, "Give me a group of honest fellows—even inexperienced and unlettered—but thoroughly honest souls, and I will give you a good administration of government." What he was saying was, "Give me the brightest and the most gifted minds in our land, and I still cannot form a sound and efficient government if they are lacking in honesty." Here was a patriot dedicated to the cause of learning as exemplified by his founding of the University of Virginia. He was not overlooking the need for knowledge through education. He knew the indispensable value of experience in public affairs. Still, he was saying to his countrymen—to reach greatness America must have a government manned by trustworthy and honorable servants in office—nothing less will do. This yardstick was the measure of good government in his day; it is no less so in this day.

Warnings of the serious impact of moral and ethical decay in the private and public sectors have been signaled from time to time.

Note with me, if you please, the comments on the Editor's Page of *U.S. News & World Report,* written by Howard Flieger, in the issue of September 29, 1975.

> If moral education is about to make a comeback, there are those who are convinced it is just in the nick of time. They trace rising crime, political chicanery, even inflation, the federal deficit and setbacks in foreign policy to a nationwide decline in moral and ethical values that have been eroding at an accelerated pace for years.
>
> The world is littered with the ruins of societies destroyed by irresponsibility. We cannot succeed by trying to treat the symptoms—crime, anger, hostility, poverty and war. We must seek the root causes and deal with them.
>
> Any signal of increasing interest in the study of morals and ethics can be taken as an indicator that today's young people do, indeed, care about such things.

Let me direct your attention to the Report of the Watergate Special Prosecution Force. I did not write this report, although most of what it contains is based on matters that came to light while I served as Special Prosecutor. But members of the staff, who saw what I saw and came to know what I had learned, wrapped up in these words what had occurred during what may be termed as the Watergate era—and some of which occurred even prior thereto. Here is what the Report says, and this part I fully approbate:

In considering what recommendations to include in this report, WSPF concentrated on what it did observe: criminal abuse of power by Government officials in high places; historical growth of secrecy in the federal executive branch unchecked by Americans and their elected Congress; unchallenged, subjective judgments by the executive branch in identifying persons and organizations that constitute an impermissible threat to the national interest and to executive policy; an undemocratic condition wherein money is power, and skillful, cynical public relations cements that power; and finally, a silent, sometimes grudging, sometimes willful conclusion by some Government representatives *that ethical standards are irrelevant because quick implementation of policy goals is mandatory*, but achievable only by social and personal injustices to others.

Well, as the Watergate Report points out, some of the wrongs and excesses of which it speaks did not begin with the so-called Watergate era. But they escalated to unprecedented heights during that time.

United States Supreme Court Justice Harry A. Blackmun, speaking at Emory University School of Law on the subject of "Thoughts About Ethics," reminded us as follows:

Fifteen months ago, at the 1973 ABA meeting in Washington, I was asked to participate at the annual Prayer Breakfast. Due to the nature of the occasion, a biblical text was indicated. I chose the story of Nehemiah. You remember the scene: the walls of Jerusalem were in ruins, despair engulfed the city, and all seemed lost and not worth the effort. I thought

> I detected somewhat similar signs in Washington—the pall of Watergate, our own "Jerusalem" figuratively in ruins. . . .
>
> It has been a time of tribulation, agony, despair, discouragement, and wonder. But the trial has not been ours alone. Much of the free world, if one but looks, seems to have been, or to be, in precarious political and ethical balance. West Germany, France, Italy, Great Britain, India, Pakistan, Greece, Cyprus, Turkey, Ireland, Ethiopia—the list goes on. Why?
>
> May I suggest, with some diffidence, that we have been and are in the midst of a wave of moral and ethical confusion. The balance has been missing. The compass has been askew. It seems that the old value guideposts are no longer there, or at least are no longer looked to and relied upon. We have been awash and we have floundered. We have retreated to discussions of situation ethics and of the "new" morality, and we have rationalized and compromised and made excuses. And, of course, we continue to flounder.
>
> Are the old indicia of proper conduct really gone or are we so self-blinded that we will not see them? Has the law lost its moral base or has it never really had one?

A periodic decline of morality in government is recorded in ancient, medieval, and modern histories. In our country it had its place of concern from the founding days, as we shall see. In current times we are inclined to associate the subject with Watergate because of the unprecedented escalation of the problem in that sphere of governmental activity. When it erupted, the spotlight was thrown on a particular phase of moral wrongdoing—to a greater extent than ever before.

Certainly, I have known nothing during my adult lifetime to equal the shocking disclosures of recent years, and I suppose that this is true with most of you. Naturally, this causes us to pause and wonder whether we have been indifferent to shady practices, to corrupt dealings, to dishonest conduct in government. Have we become callous and hardened in sensibility to such conduct—falling victim to the thoughts expressed by Alexander Pope when he reminded us:

> Vice is a monster of so frightful mien,
> As to be hated needs but to be seen;
> Yet seen too oft, familiar with her face,
> We first endure, then pity, then embrace.

Or is a lesser indictment more appropriate—have our daily lives been so preoccupied with other affairs that we could no longer take inventory of the conduct of those to whom we entrust the affairs of government? Have we been so apathetic as no longer to have expressed reactions of indignation when we learned of questionable conduct? Could it be that we have been so absorbed in materialism and in our individual welfare and success that we could not bother to register protestations and outcries to acts of improprieties and overreaching and plain dishonesty by public officials? Or could it be that finally there has been a public awakening to the cancerous growth of dishonesty in public office, leading to stricter investigations and enforcement measures?

Of all of the Watergate era aftermaths, none surprised me more than the attitude of a segment of our citizens who could not be bothered by, or even impressed with, the revelations of this great trauma that beset our nation. With a brush-off wave of arm or a shrug of the shoulders, it was not uncommon to hear the remarks "It has been going on for a long time" or "It did not begin with Watergate." Actually, some shoddy transgressions did presage Watergate as is pointed out in the Watergate Special Prosecution Force Report of October 1975. Let me quote one brief passage: "Many of the Watergate phenomena had their historical precedents. Many had grown with no deterrence from other branches of Government. Others had grown without questions from the people and from the press."

How long practices of the general nature of Watergate may have been going on—to a greater or lesser or to the same degree—is not even a mitigating circumstance in assessing the gravity of the lawbreaking that occurred in that sordid episode. If there were prior instances of wrongdoing in the Executive Branch, whether to a worse, lesser, or the same degree, is really beside the point in evaluating the shocking conduct there revealed. Let us assume that there were prior instances of grave infractions of law and probity. Why were these instances not brought to light, and why were the offenders not called to an accounting for their wrongs? The answer would have to be that they were condoned and permitted to serve as a spawning ground for subsequent misdeeds, either because of the lack of vigilance in ascertaining their existence, or because of indolence in doing nothing about them.

A commission appointed by President Ford caused a Task Force to study the subject of "public conduct." The charge given the Task Force bluntly stated: "One of the critical challenges before our country today is the restoration of the public's faith in equality and integrity of government." It further stated that "the maintenance of this confidence depends primarily on the quality of the men and women attracted to the public service and *the public's trust in the processes of government.*"

Under the heading "Philosophy of the Report" the Task Force, reporting late in 1976, said: "The polls show clearly that public respect for government officials has declined sharply in recent years." It further stated: "We regard the problem as serious."

Coeval with the preparation of this lecture, there appeared on our national horizon another example of questionable morality in government. The latest episode involves the presidency and is now in the process of investigation. Regardless of whether any laws were violated in the process, moral and ethical principles may well have been circumvented.

No one knew better than the President that his brother Billy, expert though he may have been as a peanut raiser and gasoline seller, had no expertise in industrial, technological, or governmental affairs. He had nothing to offer to Libya except a willingness to misuse his relationship to the President of the United States. Used properly and ethically, his kinship to the President had no value to Libya. Used improperly and unethically, it could conceivably result in favors that country was seeking.

For many months—ever since Billy Carter was consorting publicly with the Libyans and boasting of his friendship with their leaders—the President was forewarned of the dangers to the institution of the presidency inherent in his brother's close association with these characters of questionable design. But the President did nothing officially—nothing to contain this potential danger of impropriety. He could and should have issued a public statement either at a press conference or by other means defining the position of the White House. "My brother, Billy Carter, is now representing the government of Libya," he should have announced. "In so doing, he is to be accorded the same rights and privileges as any other American who has become an agent of a foreign country—but none greater. To avoid any misunderstanding or any intimation that special privileges are expected, this statement is issued."

Such a public pronouncement was not only indicated—it was essential—because of the involvement of a nation rightfully suspect in the minds of Americans.

Instead, in the exercise of extremely poor judgment, the President encouraged Billy's efforts by sending him a State Department message praising Billy's conduct in Libya, to which the President appended his words of commendation on how well Billy did under "dry" circumstances.

The president should have known that monetary considerations would be involved and that his brother, who was hanging on the ropes of bankruptcy, would not be serving the interests of Libya for "peanuts." And whether the large sum of money to pass hands was an outright payment or in the guise of a loan is entirely beside the point. The entire transaction was morally wrong.

Business, as well as government, has come under widespread criticism in recent years because of a lack of moral probity. The Consumers Agency Act—another proposed yoke for the businessman to carry—almost became legislation at a prior session of Congress simply because some of Ralph Nader's forces and other groups of that order were able to point to actual transgressions of ethical conduct on the part of some business interests. From the showing of these transgressions, they argued that widespread regulation through the passage of this Act was necessary. It behooves both industry and the professions to avoid these self-inflicted wounds.

I would suggest that in a matter of business morality and ethics, business interests should be exercising a special care to keep their house in good order. Improperly undertaking to influence public officials should never be a part of lobbying practices. "It takes two to tango" is an old saying, and if improper payments are not tendered to public officials—there will be no recipients to go wrong and to disgrace the public office. The General Services Administration representatives, by way of example, would not have betrayed their trust had there not been business representatives providing the inducement.

I have long wanted to talk on the subject of the habit we have in our country of treating neglect with a reaction so drastic as to make the remedy unduly burdensome. What intrigues me—often saddens me—is how we swing our pendulum of life in an arc of 180 degrees, seldom stopping at the more reasonable 90 degree mark or at any other suitable point in between.

Let us take a few illustrations occurring in recent years. After long ignoring some questionable practices in the obtaining of campaign contributions as well as other improprieties, when Watergate came along, it was a signal that we must become ever so righteous, and this caused the unleashing of all sorts of reforms in the making and acceptance of campaign contributions, some of which make good sense and others of which do not. There were cries for remedial action, including that of the appointment of a permanent special prosecutor which, incidentally, I consider to be both unnecessary and questionable as to constitutionality. The general reaction in Washington to Watergate became so extreme that some public officials even became concerned about holding closed door conferences for fear of criticism or investigation.

When finally the General Services Administration irregularities came to light involving dozens of individuals and untold instances of kickbacks and other forms of corruption, there followed a rush to tighten regulations, some of which were burdensome and totally unnecessary.

A GAO Task Force for the Prevention of Fraud has been directed to concentrate its efforts of review and evaluation of procedures and controls in the following government agencies:

—Labor Department's Comprehensive Employment Training Act's programs,
—Community Services Administration,
—Small Business Administration,
—Naval Materiel Command.

A toll-free number allowing citizens to report instances of fraud (800/424-5454).

Appointment in all major agencies of Inspectors General to oversee agency-wide antifraud programs.

More attention paid to requirements for periodic program compliance checks.

Prosecutors and investigators experienced in fraud cases are being assembled to develop improved detection and investigation techniques and to identify program weaknesses.

Naturally, the question arises, "Why was not just one of these countermeasures introduced and used prior to the revelation of these widespread acts of corruption? Is this not a clear admission that indifference and inattentiveness had taken place? And why unleash all of these supposedly corrective forces in one big swoop without first determining the effectiveness and need of each?

Let me direct your attention to a recent article in the *Wall Street Journal* on the subject of "Business Ethics and Economic Man."

> Business ethics, in any civilization, is properly defined by moral and religious traditions, and it is a confession of moral bankruptcy to assert that what the law does not explicitly prohibit is therefore morally permissible. Yet, curiously enough, this is what businessmen often seem to be saying—therewith inevitably inviting government to expand its code of prohibitions. And the reason this has happened is that businessmen have come to think that the conduct of business is a purely "economic" activity, to be judged only by economic criteria, and that moral and religious traditions exist in a world apart, to be visited on Sundays perhaps.

Private industry must realize that the quickest way to invite regulations on top of regulations is for antibusiness interests to be able to point to breaches of good ethics—to moral wrongdoing—on the part of business institutions. Some of the regulatory burdens saddled on business are caused by public reaction to questionable business practices—even though resorted to by relatively few.

The American Assembly was founded by Dwight D.

Eisenhower in 1950 when he was president of Columbia University. It holds meetings and publishes books to illuminate issues of United States policy. W. Averill Harriman made a gift of the meeting place—Arden House—which has been described as a "site for undisturbed consideration of major public questions." Last year the American Assembly conducted a meeting on "corporate governance." In their final report the participants expressed dislike for centralized government power as a remedy for concentrated private power within the corporation. They stressed ideas for nongovernmental oversight by such groups as directors and auditors and by efforts at self-regulation and changes in management practice. They concluded, however, that "if private initiatives fail, the issues of corporate governance are important enough that government will have to address them."

They also reached an agreement that companies, among other things, "should improve their responsiveness to emerging . . . ethical questions."

In its August issue of last year, *Fortune Magazine* in an article by Arthur M. Louis made a point which is well for all corporate executives to remember. The article says:

> The success of a corporation nowadays depends not only on how it makes and markets its products, but also on how it is perceived by the public. Members of Congress, government agencies, consumer groups, and the press are all scrutinizing business with an intensity and zeal rarely displayed in the past. Some of the scrutineers are bound to be hostile toward corporations—which makes it all the more

important that businessmen exert every effort to demonstrate that their motives and actions meet the highest standards.

Frederick H. Stinchfield, noted Minneapolis lawyer and president of the American Bar Association forty-three years ago, delivered an address on the subject of "What Leaders Should Live and Lead By," and here is what he said in part:

> What is this honor, a high sense of which we should cultivate? It embraces many characteristics; but primarily its basis must be one of sincerity. It must mean that advice to the many shall be frank, honest, sincere and accurate; all of which requires that words, whether printed or spoken, must always be used to convey truth; and to convey the truth, no matter how unpleasant it may be to those who listen or however unfortunate may be the immediate reaction upon the speaker. The honorable man or woman must use words, not with any primary purpose of pleasing his hearers, to lull them into a false sense of security, to unfairly arouse their hopes, or to create faith in an immediate and happy solution of their difficulties, when in fact only a lesson of self-sacrifice can be the teaching which will relieve the hearers from their misfortunes. There is no place, in the mouth of the honorable man, for words of persuasion that are misstatements of fact. Nor can such a man give reasons for his conclusions which he believes unsound, excusing himself because hearers, pleased, will be more readily induced to action. The honest man will give to others what the speaker believes, not what is easy for the hearers to accept. Some day

> people will have learned that it is not words that immediately please, upon which dependence should be placed, but words which have in them reality, truth and sincerity. You will see that my immediate concern is that too unique quality which we term intellectual honesty. We confine ourselves, for the time being, to a consideration of honor in the use of words; our power with words is made possible by education. Few others have it. It is our wealth; and it is our duty to use it honestly.

It seems to me that this is a good note on which to close.